A
Russian
Princess
Remembers

DOUBLEDAY

NEW YORK   LONDON   TORONTO   SYDNEY   AUCKLAND

A
Russian
Princess
Remembers

THE JOURNEY FROM TSARS TO GLASNOST

Ekaterina Meshcherskaya

TRANSLATED BY ALYONA KOJEVNIKOV

Except for the two photographs credited to Vadim Krokhin, all the other photographs in this book are from the author's own personal archives.

Portions of this book originally published in Russian under the title Trudovoe Khreshchenie, Novy Mir, No. 1, 1988.

PUBLISHED BY DOUBLEDAY
a division of Bantam Doubleday Dell Publishing Group, Inc.
666 Fifth Avenue, New York, New York 10103

DOUBLEDAY and the portrayal of an anchor
with a dolphin are trademarks of Doubleday,
a division of Bantam Doubleday Dell Publishing Group, Inc.

Library of Congress Cataloging-in-Publication Data

Meshcherskaya, Ekaterina.
   A Russian princess remembers : the journey from tsars to
glasnost / Ekaterina Meshcherskaya. — 1st ed.
      p.   cm.
   ISBN 0-385-26136-5 :
   1. Meshcherskaya, Ekaterina. 2. Soviet Union—Princes and
princesses—Biography. 3. Soviet Union—History—
Revolution, 1917–1921. 4. Soviet Union—Social conditions—
1917– I. Title.
DK254.M45A3   1989
947.084'092—dc19
[B]   89-32038
                                                             CIP

ISBN 0-385-26136-5
Translation copyright © 1989 by
Doubleday, a division of Bantam
Doubleday Dell Publishing Group, Inc.

All Rights Reserved
Printed in the United States of America
July 1989
FIRST EDITION
BG

Contents

Part I Baptism by Hard Work   vii

1   BROTHER VYACHESLAV AND THE PALACE TOWER   1

2   "NO JOBS FOR PRINCESSES"   9

3   DEFLATING THE "DARLING OF
     ST. PETERSBURG SOCIETY"   22

4   RUBLEVO: THE COOK'S DAUGHTER   30

5   MAKING MUSIC, EARNING MY KEEP   44

6   MAMA'S SECRET GIFT   65

7   MAMA AND THE THREE "CRIMINALS"   86

Part II Father and Mother   99

8   MY FATHER'S DAUGHTER LILY AND
     THE ITALIAN CONNECTION   101

9   THE WODZINSKYS AND THE PODBORSKYS   1 1 5

10   ENTER PRINCE MESHCHERSKY   1 2 2

11   KATYA, MAESTRO BIMBONI, AND LA SCALA   1 4 8

12   "UNEXPECTEDLY AND FOREVER"   1 6 4

13   DAYS AT VESELY PODOL   1 8 8

14   THE PRINCE'S LEGACY   2 0 6

Part III Epilogue   2 1 3

Part I
Baptism by Hard Work

1
Brother Vyacheslav and the Palace Tower

*M*y childhood recollections are fragmentary and unconnected, but I know that my earliest years were spent on our estate, Vesely Podol, in the Khorolsk district, Poltava province, in the Ukraine. This was my mother's favorite estate, for here she had spent the first years of her happy marriage. The palace on the estate consisted of forty-five large rooms, and I recall brilliant expanses of inlaid parquet floors, sunlight streaming in through numerous windows, and, far beyond those windows, the blue expanse of a large lake, its waves dancing in the sun and the bobbing white sails of skiffs.

My first tactile memory is the pleasant feeling of soft velvet on my chin and elbows. That was the red velvet upholstery of the benches in the ballroom. I wanted to rub my chin on each and every one of them, but a stern voice bade me stop, and a firm hand pulled me away from this agreeable pastime. As my chin and elbows barely reached the seats of the benches, I must have been very small at the time.

That same firm hand would propel me on many occasions to hide from our nanny or governess behind a stuffy row of dresses at the back of a wardrobe, behind the large rolls of carpet stored in the pantry, or under the graceful curves of the palace stairs. Sometimes that hand would guide me into one of the huge dog kennels, where it was hot and smelled of animal fur and where an enormous, blue-eyed wolfhound licked my nose hospitably with his wet, pink tongue. Winding my fingers in his white and brown spotted coat, I would freeze into immobility behind his broad back.

That mighty hand belonged to the ruler of my childhood destiny, my older and only brother, Vyacheslav. Demanding unquestioning obedience, he led me into all sorts of scrapes, taught me how to hoodwink the adults and then how to maintain silence "unto death" when interrogated.

The huge park, the greenhouses with rare plants, flowers and fruits, the palace's indoor "winter garden," and the palace itself afforded us, incorrigible scamps that we were, endless opportunities for mischief. But our youthful curiosity centered, first and foremost, on the palace tower. Because of its height, we were forbidden to enter the tower unless accompanied by adults.

Oh, that tower! It drew us like some siren song, and to us it was the most important feature of the palace. The tower was a full four stories high, with a small fifth level equipped as an observatory and containing, apart from a telescope, a multitude of instruments and containers the use and purpose of which was a total mystery to us. The tower had been built in the Gothic style, with four smaller towers superimposed on its sides. It was topped by a steeply angled roof, surmounted by a pennant-shaped rotating weathervane. The tower stood there like a proud sentinel with the Meshchersky coat of arms on its breast.

But forbidding anything to Vyacheslav was a waste of effort. Apart from an ironbound door opening from the hallway—normally kept locked—there was a secret entrance to the tower. A narrow underground passage led directly from a greenhouse to a small door hidden by a thick curtain of climbing hops. Enlisting the aid of our blacksmith's son, a youth called Osip, Vyacheslav had long ago found a key that would unlock this door. In exchange, he gave Osip his big penknife. Nobody noticed this door because it never entered anybody's head to use the secret passageway, which had been dug for some reason by the palace's earlier owners, the Kochubey princes. As a precaution, Vyacheslav never carried the key on him, but kept it hidden in one of the big decorative urns on the terrace. Very, very rarely, and only in the absence of adults, especially his French tutor, Dudant, did Vyacheslav venture into the tower. Even more rarely did he take me with him. The tower contained a fencing room with rapiers and sabers, mesh facemasks, and thick leather breast guards. There was also a gym room with swings, climbing frames, a wooden vaulting horse, and a rotating boxing dummy. On another floor there was a billiard room, a room with a fireplace, a round chamber full of models of knights in armor, weapons of all kinds on the walls, ancient saddles, stuffed birds and animals, and many, many other wonders which have slipped from my memory.

My brother always regretted that he was followed into the world by a sister and not by another boy. He decided to make the best of it, however, and felt himself obliged to shape my character. Occasionally his methods were very cruel. But in his own way he was very fond of me, and I did my best to live up to his standards. He certainly did a good job in driving all vestiges of feminine timidity and helplessness out of me.

This is how he taught me my first lesson.

That memorable July day was hot and oppressive. All the adults, including our French and German governesses, had driven off in carriages or had gone on horseback early that morning to visit the owners of the neighboring estate, the Counts Miloradovich. Because I was considered too young to go along, I was left behind, and Vyacheslav remained too, as punishment for some misdemeanor. I was to be in the care of my nanny,

Pashenka, and Vyacheslav was supposed to be under the eye of his tutor. He had been ordered to translate a whole chapter of *Robinson Crusoe* from Russian into French.

The sun beat down mercilessly. It was airless, humid, and difficult to breathe. All the signs were that a storm was imminent. The silk curtains had been drawn, making the air inside the rooms look golden. The palace was virtually empty, and there was nobody in the park. Instead of the usual waves, there was a kind of choppy ripple on the lake's surface, making it look like an old, dull mirror. A skiff, sails hanging limply, was tied up at the jetty. Before lunch I played near the terrace with my dolls, while Pashenka sat nearby with some sewing. Tired by the heat, she tended to drowse. Vyacheslav was not there; he was working on his translation in the schoolroom under the supervision of his tutor. Then lunch was served on the terrace: soft-boiled eggs, cottage cheese with sour cream, and "varenets"—fermented boiled milk chilled on ice. After lunch it was customary to take an hour's rest. Nanny Pashenka settled me down in the nursery and went off for a nap in her own room.

I was awakened by someone shaking my shoulder— Vyacheslav. He motioned me to keep quiet, helped me put on my dress, and did up the buttons at the back. "Where's Dudant?" I whispered.

He didn't answer but, as usual, hauled me along by the hand.

"In the flurry when they left," he hissed rather than whispered, "they forgot to lock the door to the tower. There's going to be a storm. We'll go up to the observatory and watch the lightning flashes through the telescope."

Partly from fear and partly from running down the corridors and hiding from the servants around corners and behind doors, I was soon gasping for breath.

"Stop puffing like a railroad train!" hissed Vyacheslav again.

It's true I was breathing very heavily and was on the point of tears. I was frightened. I dreaded watching the storm. I had never seen one in my life, because every time there was a storm, Pashenka made sure I was protected from it, as was the practice in those days. She would take me to my snug nursery, close the heavy oak shutters, and the room would be plunged into semi-darkness relieved only by the sanctuary lamp flickering before the icons. Nanny would quickly light a candle saved from the Divine Liturgy on Easter night and begin to whisper a prayer. Then she would sit in the armchair and hide my head in her lap, covering my ears with a warm hand every time there was a clap of thunder. This was very cozy and not at all frightening, even though I knew there were whistling winds and torrential rains outside. Nanny's dress always smelled of cinnamon, cardamon, and nutmeg, which meant that she would soon pull a cookie for me out of her pocket. The cookie would be given in secret, so that neither my governess nor any of the adults would know, because Nanny was not supposed to give me any snacks. This small, shared secret made me feel very happy, and the light of the sanctuary lamp, reflected in the icon casing, lulled me into drowsiness.

But now, what horrors awaited me? Vyacheslav towed me inexorably forward, forward. . . .

As it emerged later, Vyacheslav's French tutor had said that on that day he would go swimming rather than take a rest after lunch. This was a standard maneuver of his, for he leaped at any excuse to make his way to the servants' quarters, where there was a separate building for the young female staff. Our Frenchman, enchanted by the beauty of these young Ukrainian girls and charmed by their singing, would stand under their windows for hours on end. On more than one occasion, they doused him with cold water from a window, soaking him from head to foot. So on this occasion, too, he headed off in their direction.

While my brother and I were making our way to the coveted door it became so dark that it seemed as though night had fallen. The sky was completely obscured by threatening clouds, and a strong, sharp wind sprang up, gusting around the palace. As we climbed up the tower stairs, I summoned up enough courage to ask Vyacheslav, "What if they come back home? What then?"

"We'll escape through the secret tunnel," he replied confidently. "I've got the key. We'll say that we were out in the garden."

"But what if . . ." I began, meaning to point out that nobody was likely to believe that we had gone out into the park in a storm and in pouring rain, but Vyacheslav interrupted me contemptuously.

"What if . . . what if . . ." he mimicked. "Are you scared or something?"

Scrambling up the stairs in his wake, I comforted myself with the hope that the storm might not kill us and that Vyacheslav would, as usual, lift me up to sit on the green baize of the billiard table. I would roll the billiard balls around trying to get them into the pockets, and Vyacheslav would try on pieces of armor or do acrobatics on the swing in the gym room: that was how we usually spent our time when we managed to go into the tower.

Alas, my hopes were in vain. As we climbed higher and higher, I could see martins and swallows flying around frenziedly outside. Every peal of thunder seemed closer than the last. Fierce flashes of lightning bathed the walls of the tower in a weird, bluish-violet light. When we paused on one of the landings, I looked out a window and saw the thick branches of trees thrashing back and forth, like the hands of a giant begging for help. Even the poplars, always so proud and straight, were moving from side to side, as though rebuking or threatening.

I panicked. In the wavering light cast by the flashes of lightning, it seemed to me that one of the suits of armor had started to come to life. A thunderclap deafened me. Rain dashed against the windows, driven by mighty gusts of wind. It seemed as though someone was emptying huge tubs of water over the tower. As we reached the door to the observatory, another clap of thunder made me plop down onto the floor. I seized my brother's hand and began to scream at the top of my voice, "I'm not going any further! Let's go back! I'm scared!"

He tried to drag me further; I resisted with all my might, bit his hand as hard as I could, and, continuing to scream, began stamping my feet.

In a flash, Vyacheslav darted over to a window, flung it open, leapt back to me, seized me under the arms, and, holding me like that, climbed out onto the window sill. I could not wrench myself out of his vicelike grip and kept screaming. He stood up on the window sill and made a slight movement, as though he were about to throw me out. I hung in midair, held only by his hands. Bluish-black clouds scudded across the sky over my head. Rain lashed my face, my ears, my eyes. The steely grip under my arms hurt terribly. . . . Choking from the rain, I stopped my screaming, and then everything went black. . . .

I recovered to find myself sitting on the floor under the still-open window. Vyacheslav was bending over me, wiping my wet face and hair with his handkerchief. He was smiling and would suck his hand occasionally, which was bleeding from my bite.

"Well, scaredy-cat?" he said, patting my cheek. "Tell me, are you ever going to be a coward again and be frightened of a storm?"

I was unable to utter so much as a word. My dress, which was soaked through, clung to me and hampered movement. Everything around us still boomed and shook, the lightning still flashed, but I was no longer afraid. I sat there and watched the water streaming off my clothes form a puddle on the floor.

Vyacheslav lifted me by the scruff of the neck as though I were a puppy, but seeing that I could barely stand on my feet, quickly hoisted me up onto his back.

"Hold tight!" he ordered.

I clasped my arms around his neck and pressed my face into his cheek. Slowly, he began to go down the stairs. "Nanny Pashenka will change your clothes now. We'll go and wake her. Mind you, she's probably already running around the place looking for us. Tell her that we went out onto the terrace because you wanted to stand in the rain for a bit. Got that? She wouldn't tell on us anyway. As for you, if you want me to love you and count you my sister, you'll have to be brave. Remember, there's nothing worse than being a coward. It's a pity we didn't get into the observatory, but never mind . . . today was your first test for courage."

Since that day I have never been afraid of storms.

2
"No Jobs for Princesses"

The Revolution was upon us. The aristocracy proved to be the least prepared for it. The greater part of the aristocracy had no interest in politics and took no part in it. Of course, everyone knew that there were revolutionaries who occasionally threw bombs. There was a general belief that "a Constitution is being drafted which will limit the powers of the tsar through the institution of a parliament," and that was that. For such people, the Revolution really did come like the proverbial bolt from the blue. They felt themselves buffeted by an unexpected hurricane; it was as though they had been caught by a tempest in an open field where, deafened by thunder and drenched by pouring rain, they scurried around, dazed, searching for shelter and rescue from the deadly, burning bolts of lightning.

"I will not go anywhere," declared our mother. "I have no intention of going around to the foreign embassies, cap in hand, asking for protection from my own country."

There was not a family the Revolution had not split. Friendships which had withstood the test of years and seemed unshakable now came adrift, family ties were sundered. This tragedy did not bypass our family, either. Mama's pride and joy, her favorite child, her only son, my brother Vyacheslav, left Russia.

Several years later, when we received our first letter from Vyacheslav from abroad, my mother had no qualms about casting off her own son forever. She wrote him a few terrible, painful words: "You have forgotten about love for the Motherland—you have left your native land, so now you can forget about the mother and sister you left there . . ." My mother would never accept compromises of any kind.

Of course the times were not easy for us. Even now, it is hard for me to write about our life. When you write about painful subjects, it is vital to be objective, precise, to avoid coloring events and distorting the truth. Our lot was particularly difficult because, apart form our birth and wealth, we stood in the shadow of seven centuries of the Meshchersky crest, and all the hatred and distrust our class had earned among the common people lay upon us like a pall. But my fearless mother remained undaunted.

There were many among the aristocracy who withdrew into themselves, seethed with hostility, and sought to shut themselves off from all and sundry. Furtively, they sold off valuables on the black market, without thinking that this could not go on indefinitely. And indeed, several years later, after all that could be sold had been, you would see them in Stoleshnikovy Lane, dirty, bedraggled, and debased, begging for alms in perfect French. It was a shameful and repulsive sight. Thus were people's true natures exposed.

When our so-called friends abused and reproached my mother for her readiness to go along with all the changes in the country and keep peace with "that rabble," she would reply, "I do not yet understand the new life or the new government, but they embody the will of the people. That is what I believe."

People were really quite extraordinary in those days and

their ardent hearts cast an aura of romance over the first post-revolutionary years. The days flew past, and how many fascinating yet unrecorded moments and images whirled by into oblivion!

When banks were nationalized, the opening up of safes posed great problems for the inexperienced people who had been charged with this task and who were to be responsible for the treasures contained therein. A special appeal was published, calling upon the owners of safe-deposit boxes in the banks to come forward with their keys. It was stated that part of the owners' "decorative trivia" (jewelry with colored precious stones) could be retained. In those days, the state was in desperate need of foreign currency, so the government was interested in acquiring only gold, not precious stones. It is hard to describe the ensuing uproar. Rumor multiplied upon rumor and gave rise to hundreds of wild fears.

"Have you heard? Do they think we're all fools? Am I to hand over my property to them with my own hands?" cried some.

"Yes, we know what his really means," sneered others, nodding sagely. "You turn up, hand them the key, and that will be the last anyone will see of you!"

"It's just the latest Bolshevik trick," whispered still others. "That's all!"

And the vast majority stayed away from the banks with their safe-deposit-box keys. "Let the bastards break in! Let them reduce the building to rubble!" they hissed vindictively.

My mother was one of the few to obey the government edict and go. I believe she was motivated by her innate sense of decency. Unfortunately, she did not take me with her on that day, so I can give no firsthand account. Rather than indulge in surmise, I shall merely repeat what I have heard my mother tell me on numerous occasions.

The bank was surrounded by a cordon of soldiers. They were only allowing through those who had proof of identity and their safe keys on them. Armed guards were posted on every floor of the building, and there was an "operative group" for each floor, too. The nationalization of gold in the part of the bank where our safe-deposit box was located was being handled by a man wearing a sailor's uniform. It was said that he had come down from Petrograd. For some reason, no specialists or jewelers were present. The sailor had an ammunition belt slung across his chest and wore a hip holster with a huge revolver. Young, broad-shouldered, and wide-eyed, he was clearly very conscious of the responsibility given him and tried to keep his open, kindly face looking stern and official. He had no idea of the value of any jewelry, all he knew was that the state needed gold. An array of scales stood on tables between the safes.

When my mother unlocked our safe, the sailor started scooping out handfuls of gold artifacts and dropping them on the scales: men's and women's watches with their chains, cigar cases, lockets, medallions. Someone had obviously told him that the personal monogrammed clips worn at court by ladies-in-waiting were made out of diamonds, so the clips belonging to all who had been ladies-in-waiting in our family were put in a cup on a separate set of scales. Crosses, chains, and wedding rings went on yet another scale. After that, the sailor turned his attention to engraved gold cups and goblets. He was assisted by a thin, elderly man in civilian clothes. This man was constantly racked by a deep cough and seemed to be there because he was literate. He was completely engrossed in weights and measures. From time to time, he would enter elaborate figures into a thick ledger, carefully inserting a piece of carbon paper between its pages.

Finally, the sailor stood back and contemplated the considerable piles of valuables on the scales before him. Then he scooped up everything else that remained and, with a careless gesture, pushed it to the end of the table. "Here," he said to my mother, who stood in stunned silence, "you can keep all these bits and pieces." Motioning her to clear the table, he handed her a receipt to sign.

What a pity that I, who was still a silly adolescent in those days, never felt any interest in that piece of paper and took no pains to preserve it! It was only years later that I realized the value of this fascinating historical document. All I remember is that it named a sum equivalent to the value of the gold objects requisitioned from us, and below that were the words: "Small items covered with precious stones—costume jewelry—issued to Citizeness E. P. Meshcherskaya, as having no currency value."

The sailor had become particularly incensed over what we called the Othello necklace. This piece was made of fine gold mesh and studded with rubies linked by pearls. The necklace had been specially made to hold a miniature of great beauty, a depiction of Othello, about the size of a fifteen-kopeck coin. A tear-shaped pearl was attached to the base of the miniature.

After studying this ensemble for a while, the sailor exclaimed angrily, "Just goes to show how shameless those upperclass women were! Going around with pictures of niggers around their necks!" He spat in disgust and threw the necklace on to the pile with the rest of the "bits and pieces." In this pile, too, was the Meshchersky family diamond, a twenty-carat rhombic stone of perfect color and clarity, in a diamond-encrusted platinum setting on a beautiful, delicate platinum chain.

This diamond was the cause of a very interesting incident. It happened during a performance of *Life for the Tsar* in the Bolshoi Theater, with Fyodor Chaliapin singing. The dowager empress, Maria Fyodorovna (Nicholas II's mother), was in the royal box. My parents were in box number thirteen, which we always rented. On that evening, my mother wore no jewelry other than the Meshchersky diamond. During the first interval, one of the empress' closest ladies-in-waiting came to our box. Speaking very pleasantly and quietly, she asked if Mother would be kind enough to remove the diamond, as the dowager empress was not wearing anything comparable that evening. Obeying etiquette, Mother took off the diamond and put it away in her reticule. But my parents then had to get up and leave the theater immediately, for court etiquette also dictated that no lady could appear in the evening in a low-cut gown without any jewelry around her neck. To do so would be considered the height of bad taste. Later, that diamond was stolen from us.

After my mother had signed the receipt proffered by the sailor, she stood stock-still, staring at the valuables she was to retain. Not expecting such an outcome, she had not brought anything in which she could put her unexpected bounty. The sailor clearly understood the reason for her confusion and handed her the small metal coffer which had held the monogrammed ladies-in-waiting pins. This coffer was like a small suitcase, consisted of three partitions, and was quite roomy.

"Go on, put 'em here," he said good-naturedly. "Show the paper and documents downstairs when you leave."

In those days, we had no real idea of the value of the articles in that chest. We had lost our three estates and two palaces. We had surrendered our Botticelli painting of the Madonna (worth half a million rubles at that time) to Felix Edmundovich Dzerzhinsky, the head of the Cheka and a protector until his death in 1926. It seemed to us that we had lost absolutely everything. All these material losses counted for nothing, though, by comparison with the loneliness we felt, having lost all our relatives on both Father's and Mother's sides. Soon we also lost our apartment on Povarskaya (now Vorovskovo) Street in the house belong to my godmother, Alexandra Alexandrovna Miloradova. Then, in view of our "princely" origins, we were refused permission to reside in Moscow.

We wandered around, homeless, seeking shelter for the night from our acquaintances. Many of them, remembering my mother's numerous kindnesses to them in the past, would put us up for a while. But such occasions became less and less fre-

quent, and our friends' faces grew increasingly glum. Nobody
was willing to run the risk of associating with us; they were
afraid for themselves. "It's the neighbors," they would explain
lamely. "They notice everything . . ."

"It's not that we can't spare the space," others would say.
"As far as we're concerned, you could sleep here every night,
and welcome. But you know the old saying: 'Tell me who your
friends are, and I will tell you who you are' . . ."

"You know how fond we are of you, and that we trust you
implicitly," still others would say, with tears in their eyes, "but
you are princesses! You should be trying to get away from here
as quickly as possible, before it's too late. And we could be
arrested because of you, too, and then what would happen to
our children?"

And so, after tramping from door to door in search of a
corner to spend the night, we would find ourselves out in the
street again with our metal case of jewelry. On we would go,
along the well-known and well-loved streets of Moscow. When
we finally ran out of places to ask, we started bedding down at
railway stations. Nobody was interested in our valuables. Russia
was in the grip of famine and typhus. A piano could be exchanged for a handful of rye or a few potatoes. Pillows, blankets,
and sheets could be exchanged for a loaf of fragrant Ukrainian
bread from the sharp dealers who rode the trains, but we had
no bed linen to trade. All we had was a metal case full of "bau-
bles" nobody wanted.

"Mama," I asked, "why don't you write about us to Felix
Edmundovich? Remember, he promised to help us!" (Dzerzhinsky had acknowledged our patriotism in surrendering a painting
of the Madonna by Botticelli and in his capacity as head of the
Cheka was in a position to be a powerful patron.)

"Because he has more important things to worry about than
our problems," replied Mama sternly. "I will only appeal to him
as a last resort. People should cope with their own troubles."

And she explained our new position to me something like this: the wheel of history has turned, and we shall be crushed by it unless we find our place in the new order. And that is bound to be difficult.

The Moscow intelligentsia did not want to "work for the Bolsheviks" in those days. Yet work there was aplenty, especially for educated people. Still, we did not benefit from that fact. In vain, my mother haunted the labor-exchange offices, pointing out that she could be of use with her fluent knowledge of French, German, and Italian, that she had completed training as a singer and made her debut in Milan at La Scala . . .

"There are no jobs for princesses," she was told, "and we're not going to enter a princess on our books."

Nor was there any question about continuing my education. I had been studying in Moscow at an institute for daughters of the nobility near the Krasnaya Vorota. It had been a palace which Tsar Alexander III gave over for use as a girls' school as a memorial to Catherine II. This building has now been faced with gray stone, and in the first years after the Revolution it served as the headquarters of the People's Transport Commissariat (NKPS).

Our headmistress was Olga Anatolyevna Talyzin, and our patron was the marshal of the Moscow nobility, Alexander Dmitrievich Samarin. Our institute was also designated "patriotic" because it was the only one whose uniforms were in the colors of the Russian national flag: we wore white blouses, red sashes, and cornflower blue skirts.

The fall of the autocracy and the abdication of Nicholas II came to our ears in a rather unusual manner. We were all ordered to assemble in the large ceremonial hall, the walls of which were covered by portraits of tsars in heavy gilt frames. Olga Anatolyevna entered the hall, followed by our teachers and by Samarin, who was holding a sheet of paper in his hands. His old voice quavering with agitation, pausing after every sentence in an effort to suppress tears, he read us the text of Nicholas II's abdication statement. Because Olga Anatolyevna was crying and our strict, straitlaced teachers were raising handkerchiefs to their eyes, we found it all very interesting, funny, and exciting.

We were even further cheered when all the servants disappeared and we girls were sent to the kitchens to help with the preparation of meals. We had great fun stuffing ourselves full of the raw carrots and cabbage which we had been instructed to chop up. Also, we were delighted that lessons were now conducted piecemeal and haphazardly, that all the adults were frightened out of their wits, and that everything that had seemed eternal and unshakable around us was collapsing. Then hordes of Baltic Fleet sailors and armed civilians came and took over our institute. . . . That marked the end of our studies.

Those parents who had been gifted with sufficient foresight and had ordinary-sounding Russian surnames concealed their social origins and enrolled their daughters in the newly opened Soviet schools. Our teachers had agreed to continue giving instruction to a very small group of girls (including me) without payment, and the Moscow millionaire Bazilevsky made his beautiful house in the Granatny Lane available to our so-called "Teachers Association High School." This house is, nowadays, the Architects' House.

But very soon there was no more Bazilevsky, there were no more teachers, and the house was requisitioned by the state. As for me, a princess and with my name—well, no Soviet school would admit me. Such was our situation in the autumn of 1918 when Mother, with typical imperturbability, patience, and persistence, went, for the third time, to the labor-exchange office.

"Can you put me on your books as a menial worker?" Yes, they told her, that was possible. And so, one cold and rainy evening, my mother came to the Kursk railway station, where we intended to spend that night, flushed with triumph, her eyes shining.

"I've got a job!" she told me. "I'm going to work as a cook at the Rublevo waterworks. We're going there tomorrow. There's a truck leaving for Rublevo at eight o'clock every morning from Theatre Square."

"But where will we live?"

"What do you mean, where? We'll be living where the workers live. They must have some kind of housing . . ."

It was late autumn. Our clothes would become soaked with rain during the day and dried on us as we slept under cover at night. We could not undress, of course, and slept huddled together on a station bench. And now, such joy! We would have a roof over our heads, our own small corner where we could go, close the door, and know that nobody would come to drive us away . . .

We were leaving Moscow. It was a cold day, and leaden clouds hung low over the city. The drizzling rain seemed to have set in forever. I tried to appear unperturbed, but inwardly I was weeping as incessantly as the falling rain. I loved Moscow, and, despite my first joyous reaction to the news that Mother had been given a job and a roof over her head, I felt as though I were leaving Moscow, never to return. It hurt to know that there was no place for us in the city we both loved. This painful realization brought choking tears to my throat.

I dared not share this pain with my mother. I did not even dare voice my apprehensions. This was the conditioning of an aristocratic upbringing. I had been taken away from my mother at birth and turned over to a wet nurse. Then I passed into the hands of strangers whose task it was to see to my education. Thus from the very beginning I was lonesome. One day we would be in the charge of our French governess, the next day, the German one. When I was six years old, they sat me down for my first piano lesson, and a year later I began dancing lessons and learning to ride a pony in our stables. My riding instructor was an Englishman who spoke broken Russian. Afterward I was packed off to an exclusive girls' school in Moscow. We rarely saw our beautiful, strict mother. Hence we always addressed her by the formal "you" rather than the familiar "thou": we respected her, but there was no warmth in our relationship.

My mother really started talking to me only in 1917. We had been drawn closer by all that we had had to endure together, but there was still a great chasm between me, an excitable and impulsive adolescent, and this calm and self-assured woman. Neither a strict upbringing, nor iron discipline, was able to change my nature: I was born a proud and stubborn rebel, and the questions why? what for? by what right? boiled within me, especially after weathering my first personal tragedy.

The thing I valued most in life was music. I was not particularly upset when none of the newly opened Soviet schools would enroll me as a student. But when my application for admission to the conservatory was refused—"Not eligible for higher education because of her social origins" was scrawled carelessly across it—that hurt, like a nagging tooth.

I could picture the kindly face of Professor Konstantin Nikolayevich Igumnov, whom I had encountered in the street not long before. Since the age of six I had been taught music by his friend, Professor Vasili Nikolayevich Argamanov. Every three months, at the children's musical evenings, Professor Igumnov assessed the progress of his pupils, and he had given me a personal award, a bound copy of Tchaikovsky's *Twelve Months* with gold lettering on the cover. On the first page he had written in his own hand: "To Kitty Meshcherskaya for excellent progress." When we met, his long, thin face, reminiscent of some sage from an Egyptian papyrus, lit up with a smile, and from his great height he looked down at me like a friendly giant spotting a familiar pygmy.

"Kitty!" he exclaimed, "Apply immediately for entrance into the conservatory. I'll take you on. I'll get you housing in the students' quarters, and then, if you do really well, I may be able to arrange a scholarship for you. You'll be a pianist. Incidentally, I've been appointed director of the conservatory."

That "incidentally" was so typical of this unassuming, kind, and gentle man, who was such a brilliant pianist . . .

We were without a roof over our heads, on the street, not knowing where to go. In one hand, Mama carried a small bundle with our few items of clothing, in the other, the metal case full of jewelry. I clutched an armful of folders filled with Mother's and my musical notes. They were my world, these little black dots spaced out between five lines. Just by looking at them, I could hear the sound of music. This was my private kingdom, which nobody could nationalize or requisition.

I did not dare utter a syllable of this to Mother, for she was clearly of a different opinion altogether. Casting a glance at the bulging folders, I was straining to my bosom she said, coldly and disapprovingly, "What's all that for? You have no sense of priorities at all, have you? Your head is full of nothing but silly fantasies. We won't need any of that stuff in our new life."

"I'll never stop loving music!" I asserted firmly.

Mother made no reply, and I, looking at her calmly decisive face, tortured myself with dozens of unasked questions: Mama, a cook? What will people think? Will I have to be a cook, too? But I hate pots and pans! What has happened to us, and how can this be? Maybe it's all only a nightmare . . . ?

On that rainy morning we were the only passengers on the truck taking us to Rublevo. When it lumbered around the corner into the square—dark, wet, and ugly—I stared at it in fear and dislike.

"Coming to be our cook, are you?" said the cheerful, young, red-haired driver to my mother as he slung our things into the truck. Holding the case of valuables, Mama got into the cabin beside him, and I, still clutching the bundles of music, clambered onto one of the truck's huge, black tires. The driver gave me a friendly boost to help me get into the back of the truck and advised me to sit with my back to the cabin for protection from the wind. He covered me with a large sheet of canvas that had grease stains all over it and smelled strongly of gasoline. I felt quite cozy, and, if I turned sideways, I could look into the cabin and see my mother's face.

The driver stood at the front of the truck for a long time, trying to start the engine with what looked to me like a giant corkscrew, but the engine simply refused to start. Then, suddenly, it roared to life. The truck remained stationary for quite a long time, however, shuddering, backfiring, and billowing gray smoke, before it finally moved off. We were heading toward an unknown life, full of frightening secrets. . . .

Huddled under my canvas, I kept turning around to look at Mother. The head scarf she had tied around her head completely covered the glory of her luxuriant chestnut hair, and all I could see was her profile, which looked somehow strange and unfamiliar under the scarf, which she had put on for the first time that day. I loved that exquisite, cameo-like profile, which she retained to her dying day.

3
Deflating the "Darling of St. Petersburg Society"

The leading light of the so-called "golden youth" in St. Petersburg in those years was Prince Nikolai Barclay de Tolley, a strikingly handsome hussar of the Household Cavalry, whose ancestor and namesake had been a celebrated Army commander in the campaign of 1812 against Napoleon. He was the envy of all his male contemporaries. The ladies were out of their minds about him.

I was very interested in the prince because, for the life of me, I could not see why everyone was so ecstatic about him. So I watched him unobtrusively and followed him around. I did not think he was at all handsome: his looks were the picture-book kind and slightly effeminate. I tried listening to what he said and was again disappointed: there was no wit, flair, or even humor in anything he said. He spoke in banal courteous phrases and clichés, all of them boring and colorless.

For some reason not fully clear to me, I found him intensely irritating. His soft, insinuating voice seemed unnatural. I thought his mouth was too small and pink, almost feminine. His long, well-manicured fingers glittered with rings as he would lay out the cards for an intricate game of patience surrounded by a bevy of admiring elderly ladies.

"Why is he so *unreal?*" I wondered. And I wanted to sting him somehow, so that all that assumed surface layer would fall away and reveal the real person beneath.

Of course, I would have to wait for the right opportunity. In my leisure time, I composed a poem about him, this "lion of St. Petersburg society." The poem was no literary masterpiece, I knew that, but the desire to score points off this darling of high society was too strong to be suppressed. My chance came at an evening reception accompanied by dancing. Because of my age, I was, naturally, excluded from the proceedings and was sent off at nine o'clock to have my bread and milk and go to bed. Infuriating!

The dancing had been going on for some time. Happy and excited young girls flitted in and out of the ballroom to adjust their hair. Older ladies, flushed with dancing and flirtation, took the air on the balcony. Fans waved languidly to and fro, and praises of the peerless Barclay de Tolley were being sung on all sides in French. No, that was too much to bear! They had clearly all gone mad! Surely this was just the moment I had been waiting for? I must make sure that he got my poem that very evening!

First, I made a clean copy of my creation. Then, folding the paper into a small square, I hid it in my sleeve and sneaked out of the nursery. Unnoticed, I slipped into the dining room behind one of the servants. They were all scurrying back and forth, and nobody paid any attention to me. A huge table had been set, and sand-filled vases ranged down its center with bouquets of freshly cut gillyflowers, mignonettes, and many varieties of roses. I ran around the table, looking for the prince's place. At last! A place card with his name written in elaborate gold letters, surmounted by a crest. I waited for a moment when there were no servants in the room and quickly thrust the square of paper into the starched, intricate folds of his napkin. Then I scuttled out of the room, paused for a moment to catch my

breath, and then casually and innocently made my way back to
my bedroom. To Nanny's great surprise, I drank my milk quietly and obediently, then undressed and went to bed without
demur.

Needless to say, sleep was entirely out of the question. I
lay there motionless, eyes shut, doing my best to breathe quietly
and evenly so that Pashenka would think I was asleep and leave.
Soon I heard the rustle of her skirts and the soft click of the
nursery door.

My heart was hammering, seemingly in rhythm with the
poem I had written about the prince:

> *You are handsome—I agree.*
> *No one can compete with you*
> *And a great amount of grief*
> *Has been caused by your dark eyes.*
> *You are handsomer than all,*
> *Shako angled rakishly,*
> *Many sweethearts, wives and girls*
> *Have been snared inside your net.*
> *Everyone is quite amazed:*
> *Whence such devilish good luck?*
> *What's the secret? Is your air*
> *Fine enough to conquer all?*
> *The world stares, its mouth agape . . .*
> *Yet beneath the mask of beauty,*
> *There is naught but folly, coldness,*
> *And an infinite void!*

I tossed from side to side. I imagined the dancers downstairs, whirling across the floor, and turned green with envy.
How lucky they were! Dancing! They were grown-ups, so they
could do anything they liked! I waited for the first break in the
dancing. After that, everyone would go in for supper, and I
might hear an outburst of mirth when the prince found my

poem and began to read it with rising fury. But what if he was too angry to show it to anyone? Without my realizing it, sleep caught up with me and I dozed off.

I was shaken roughly awake by Vyacheslav, who loomed over me, white-faced and furious.

"You rotten little twerp!" he hissed. "Get dressed immediately, and come with me!"

"What's the matter? Where's Mama?" I asked, still half-asleep and not understanding what was happening.

"Mama . . . Mama . . ." he ground out savagely, tense with suppressed fury. "Make mischief and then head for cover, eh? Lousy sneak! I'll teach you a lesson you won't forget! Because of your moronic scribbles, His Highness has challenged Gorchakov to a duel!"

He bundled up my underclothes, my stockings, and my dress and flung them in my face.

"Come on! Move! Get them on and come with me!"

Jolted awake by the word "duel," I dressed rapidly, quaking with fear.

"Where's Mama?" I whispered again.

"She's upstairs in the card room, and she won't save you! You're going to be judged by a hussar court of honor, and after that, I'm going to beat the living daylights out of you! Come on, you rotten little sneak!"

He dragged me down the corridor, quite oblivious to the fact that my poor head was banging against walls and corners, and then gave me a mighty shove which propelled me into the officers' room.

Ah . . . ! At that moment, I forgot all about my bumps and bruises, about Vyacheslav's brutality and my fears. Everything paled before this unexpected stroke of good fortune. Here I was in the officers' room, into which girls were never admitted and which was set aside for the use of military men only. It had long been a secret ambition of mine to crop my hair, don a uniform, and be Vyacheslav's aide-de-camp when he became an officer.

And now here I was, on an equal footing with the military. What luck! What bliss!

I peered around curiously and was immediately overcome by a fit of coughing. The whole room was shrouded in a bluish haze of smoke. Then I began to make out the pattern on the carpet, the weapons hanging on the walls, a round table covered with cigarette-filled ashtrays. A card table strewn with cards stood farther back. Silver trays loaded with full and empty bottles and with glasses of all sizes lay around the room. A couple of officers were making hot punch over the embers in the fireplace at the far end of the room, balancing a cone of sugar on crossed swords and dripping rum over it from several bottles. The resulting sweet, aromatic fluid dripped into a large silver chalice which was poised over the hot embers. The air was full of the pungent smell of punch and other interesting things. Some of the officers were lounging around in armchairs, others stood in groups, talking. But as Vyacheslav and I made our entrance, all eyes turned toward the door.

There was a sudden, deathly hush.

"Go on, own up that it was you who wrote that stupid poem!" commanded Vyacheslav forcefully, prodding me in the back.

"Yes . . . it was I," I managed in a barely audible voice. Silence again. I could see that almost everyone in the room was having difficulty in suppressing grins. I glanced down and discovered that one of my stockings was sliding slowly down my leg, like a concertina. Moreover, in my hurry I had put my dress on inside-out, and its seams were sticking out in all directions.

The prince broke away from a group of officers and came over to me. Yes, now I could see that I had indeed succeeded in needling him. He had suddenly become quite plain: his face was red, he was sweating, and he kept wiping his forehead nervously with a handkerchief.

"You? You?" he repeated in amazement, coming closer and

staring at me as though seeing me for the first time. "You? But why?"

"Just because . . ."

He relaxed, the tension draining out of his face. He took me by the hand.

"Well, then, little rhymester-princess, tell me why you hate me so much?"

"I don't hate you."

"All right, let's just say that you don't like me. Tell me, what have I done to make you so angry?"

"Nothing. It was supposed to be a joke. I wanted to write an epigram, just like they used to do in Pushkin's time."

"Bit long for a epigram, isn't it? But why, little poet," he pursued, not releasing my hand, "have you taken such a dislike to me?"

"Why?" I echoed, rediscovering my courage. "Very well, I'll tell you: because everyone's in love with you, that's why!"

"Who's in love with me, in your opinion?"

"Well, there's Princess Bibi, for a start . . . but you know yourself, anyway!"

Everyone burst out laughing. Only Gorchakov remained silent and not amused. He crossed the room toward the prince and myself.

"Child," he said, looking at me sternly, "you have no idea how important your words are to me. It is a matter of honor. . . . Do you understand? Honor! I ask you to swear, here in front of everybody, that no adult—nobody at all, especially nobody in this room—had any part in composing that poem, or gave you the idea to do it."

"I swear that it was my own idea and that I did it all by myself. I wrote it in secret and didn't show it to anybody."

"So you did it just like that, off the cuff?"

"No . . . I wrote it some time ago."

"Where did you keep it until tonight?"

"In my playroom, under the carpet."

Everybody laughed again, and this time Gorchakov joined in, too. The prince kissed my hand and said, smiling, "If you were an officer, I'd challenge you to a duel!"

"When I turn sixteen, Vyacheslav is going to teach me to shoot . . ."

"No, no," he interrupted. "I am not going to wait for your sixteenth birthday, Princess, I am going to punish you straight away! And what a dreadful punishment it's going to be, too! I'm going to kiss you!"

He drew me forward, and I fought, pushing my hands against his chest. I was not strong enough to break away of course, and he planted a kiss on my cheek. I almost burst into angry tears, but then all the officers started coming up to kiss me, then took turns giving me piggyback rides around the room. Needless to say, I enjoyed myself immensely. Then they put a hussar's shako on my head and gave me a sip of hot punch. After that, they formed a circle around me.

"Three cheers for our poet!" they cried in unison. Someone lifted me up and put me in the middle of the table. They all charged their glasses and stood round the table, singing a popular hussar song: "Where are the friends of yesteryear, the brave hussars? Masters of repartee, hardheaded drinkers?"

Enraptured, I sang along with them. Before clinking glasses, each one gave me a sip from his cup. Oh, how I felt myself to be one of them! . . . Afterward they escorted me back to the nursery in procession. Tipsy from the punch and intoxicated by my success, I fell into a deep and blissful sleep.

In the morning, none of the officers gave away our secret, so the household adults knew nothing of what had passed. I was very proud of myself. For a while I even looked upon Vyacheslav with a hint of superiority, and he would shake his head, smiling ruefully. "Well, Ginger Snap!" (that was his pet name for me) "your silly prank could have caused a disaster. Everything seemed to point to Gorchakov as the author of that poem.

Just as well I took a look and recognized your handwriting, or God knows what would have happened. . . . Still, you're a great gun!"

Coming from him, there was no higher praise.

Then my memory went back to our great hall, sparkling with lights. Visitors from Petersburg were seated in a semicircle of armchairs. Among them was Grand Duke Mikhail Alexandrovich, Vyacheslav's godfather, accompanied by his adjutant, Johnston, who stood as usual a little aside, turning the pages of a book of notes on the piano. I sat on the lap of my beloved godmother, Alexandra Miloradovna. She was wearing a lilac gown and her favorite amethysts. Her plain but incredibly pleasant, mobile, and intelligent face was rather pale. She was looking directly at my mother.

It was a warm summer evening, and the large windows of the palace had been opened on to the park. A slight breeze played with the flames of the candles and stirred the crystal droplets which decorated their holders. The sweet scent of mignonettes, night jasmine, and stocks wafted in from the garden. The large Bechstein grand piano was open, making it look like a craft under a huge, black sail. Professor Igumnov, thin and angular, sat at the keyboard. In the angle formed by the top of the piano, I could see my mother. She was singing, and the beauty of her voice made my childish heart fill with happiness and soar. I could barely breathe from rapture. She was singing, her bright eyes half closed, the hint of a smile on her lips.

4
Rublevo: The Cook's Daughter

Abruptly, I was jerked back to the present. Shaking and rattling, the truck had left the environs of the city, bumped over a series of ruts and potholes, and lumbered onto a wide highway. The driver put his foot down, and we roared along. The wind tried to whip the canvas off my head, the cold rain lashed my face. The whistling of the wind and the roar of the truck's engine blended into an unspeakable din. Clutching the canvas over my head with one hand, I used the other to cradle my precious folders of notes so they wouldn't get wet and perish. From time to time I poked my head out from under the canvas to get a grip on our bundle of clothes, which tended to slide towards a corner where there was a pool of water.

I wonder what the waterworks look like? I thought, imagining something akin to a huge windmill. That "something" stood in the middle of the Moskva River and, bubbling and wheezing, scooped up water with enormous sails, straight into pipes taking it to Moscow.

But where will we live? I kept thinking. And I imagined a large, gray room, smelling like a bathhouse, with long, long pipes running around its walls. . . . My thoughts became more and more chaotic, my fantasies increasingly unreal, and eventually I fell into a kind of stupor. The cold wind immobilized me, and I could no longer maintain a grip on our bundle.

I was roused by a sharp jolt. The truck had stopped. End of the line. We had arrived in Rublevo. I had scrambled into the truck quite easily at the outset of our journey, but now I could barely straighten up. The damp and my wet clothes had stiffened my joints, and I ached abominably all over. My teeth chattered from the cold. The red-haired driver jumped up onto a wheel, grabbed me under the arms as though I were a drowning kitten, and deposited me carefully on the ground. I did not even have time to thank him properly, because he retrieved our bundle just as quickly and, paying me no further heed, lifted the hood of the truck and began poking around in the engine.

Mama told me to stay where I was while she went off to the administrative offices to "report to the management." Shivering from the cold, I fought to keep my eyes open, barely managing to hang on to the pile of sheet music. Nobody passing by paid me any attention, for which I was extremely grateful. I had been dreading the hostile, suspicious, and scornful looks which seemed inevitable when people found out who we were— members of the despised "former" nobility.

The driver continued to tinker with his motor, blowing out his cheeks, clearing something, wiping engine parts with a black, oily rag, and yet—despite his seeming absorption in his task— nodding his head this way and that, acquainting me with Rublevo. In the distance I saw the main building, the heart of the waterworks. It was a long, low structure, reminiscent of a factory, with enormous pipes towering above it. A strange, rhythmic sound emanated from this building, like a giant sighing over and over. Strangely enough, I took an immediate liking to this sound. Pointing out a larger, two-story building, the driver told me that it was the theater and social club. The symmetrically laid out brick houses in which the staff lived were called "barracks" for some reason, even though there was nothing military in their cheerful appearance. In fact, Rublevo resembled a small, neat town. Later I learned that the old, established staff of the works lived separately in gray concrete houses which were surrounded by little gardens. Many of these workers kept a cow. Rublevo was enlivened by neat avenues of carefully pruned small trees. The more I absorbed the thought that our new life would be here, the more I liked what I saw. It seemed as though we had found a little friendly haven, but deep in my heart the familiar apprehensions were already stirring: "When they find out who we are, they'll hate us!" Still, I did my best to push such disconcerting thoughts aside.

Mother returned, accompanied by a tall, strongly built man who turned out to be in charge of accommodations. He took us to one of the "barracks," climbed a flight of stairs, and flung open the door of a small, bright room with a window. The air was dry, and the floor smelled of fresh paint. The whole building had steam heating. The room had a faucet and a white porcelain washbasin. Two metal frame beds stood by the wall, and you could see clean floorboards through their springs.

"Over there," said the man, "in that red building opposite—see it?—there's boiling water available twenty-four hours a day. You can send your daughter across with a kettle, have a cup of tea, warm yourselves after the journey. If you have any problems, don't hesitate to let me know."

His manner was very friendly, and he left us to settle in. I undid our bundle, took out a large kettle, and ran across to the building he had pointed out.

A short, fast-moving queue for hot water greeted me quite affably.

"That's our new worker's daughter . . ."

"They're from Moscow . . ."

"Yes, her mother's going to be the cook here, I think . . ."

These were typical of the remarks I heard on all sides. Our

kettle, though, attracted not only attention but disapproval. We had grabbed it in a hurry when we were evicted from our apartment, and we had no other. Once it had been part of the Meshchersky silver tea service traditionally used only for one occasion: to serve tea to newlyweds on the morning after their wedding. It was an elaborate, rococo piece, with twirls and curlicues, flowers and a medallion with two cupids on it. There was a pompous, ceremonial look about it, smacking of former glories and "elegant idleness."

"Just look at that kettle! Now where would you buy something like that?"

"Fancy, ain't it . . . ?"

"That's something for folks as has nothing to do . . . Take more than an hour to clean, I shouldn't wonder! . . . Yes, surely . . ."

I filled the kettle, my face burning with embarrassment as I counted the seconds to make my escape. What would these people say if they knew that you couldn't even put this kettle on the fire because it was made of silver?

Hurrying back to our room, I reflected that my mother and I faced very difficult times ahead. Never mind the kettle, what about us, ourselves? We, living people, were also probably burdened with a wealth of unnecessary traits and features. If we could not change, we would be pitiable, but I had no idea what we would have to do in order not to alienate ourselves from these people around us. And I did want to get to know them better, to make friends with them. . . .

I tried to assume a carefree, cheerful demeanor as I entered our room.

"We'll probably have a hard time finding our house and our room at first," I said, smiling. "At the moment, all these buildings look exactly the same to me!"

"Our house? Our room?" repeated my mother slowly, as though trying to penetrate the meaning of those words; then suddenly her voice broke. She came over to me and hugged me fiercely. The unexpectedness of her touch shattered my composure. I burst into tears.

"What's going to happen to us?" I sobbed despairingly. "I'm afraid of these people, afraid of this life . . . I don't understand anything. What are we going to do?"

"There is only one thing we can do," said Mother. "We have to *believe that we will be believed*. We can live only in that hope."

I raised my head, kissed the hand with which she was wiping away my tears, and looked into her eyes. They were quite dry, but for the first time I noticed how much her delicate, lovely face had aged.

I cannot recall now why Rublevo, which was so well planned, so pleasant, with a primary and secondary school, a club, a bathhouse, and a theater, had no dining hall at the time of our arrival. Either it was being used for some other purpose or was in the process of being built, but when my mother took up her duties, the dining hall was a very long barracks, hastily thrown up out of boards. It stood far away from all the other buildings, in the middle of a windswept field. Inside, it smelled of fresh, damp timber, and its plywood door had swelled so much from steam and condensation that it would not close properly.

The kitchen was full of steam, through which one caught glimpses of huge, dark pots in which the food was cooked. Had it not been for the rattle of crockery and cutlery, the heads of the workers would have resembled disembodied angels, floating above thick white clouds. Admittedly the expressions on the faces of these "angels" were anything but serene and beatific. They were red, sweaty, and all too frequently smiling over some off-color joke.

I was astounded by the sight which met my eyes when I stuck my head around the door one morning, hoping to catch a glimpse of Mother. Here, amid constant clamor, like the muted roar of voices in a bathhouse, in the dampness, fumes, and hideous heat generated by the cooking pots, my mother was starting her working life.

Seeing me, she hurried over, seized me by the hand, and pulled me outside.

"Never! Do you hear me? Never show your face around here again!" she hissed with an anger I could not understand. "Your coming here will be misunderstood. They'll pour you a plate of soup and give you a piece of bread, thinking here's the cook's daughter, let's give her a bite to eat. When the whole country is suffering from hunger, it's a sin to waste so much as a crumb!"

"But Mama . . ." I began to remonstrate in French, then stopped short when I saw sheer terror in her face.

"Unbearable child!" she whispered fearfully. "Forget French, forget German, do you hear me? Forever! God grant that we will be able to find enough of our native Russian to explain the true reason we have remained here. Now get away from here this minute! Stay at home! I'll bring my—your—dinner in the evening."

I rushed off, burning with humiliation. The worst of it was that I could not understand what was going on. For what were we to blame? Had we done anyone any harm? Why was it forbidden to speak French or German?

Our first night in Rublevo was sheer torture. As all our clothes were soaked, we hung them up to dry on the cord which had secured my bundle of sheet music. We strung it right across the room, prying nails out of the walls, and then hammering them in where we needed them with a stone fetched from outside. In doing so, we both strained our hands. We had no mattresses or bed linen of any kind, and it was impossible to sleep on the metal springs of the beds. Finally, we decided to sleep on the floor, but we needed something to put under our heads at least. What, though? Then we remembered a pile of boards we had seen stacked up outside when we were being shown to our room. We donned our coats and went out. The boards were still there, but they were soaked with rain. We started pulling the pile apart and finally found a few boards in the middle which were only slightly damp. We neatly replaced the remaining boards, returned to our room, lay down on the floor, and put three boards, one on top of the other, under our heads. I spent a restless night, dozing off only toward morning. While I tossed and turned, I got a splinter in my ear, which swelled and became inflamed. The situation was saved by Mama's pocket manicure scissors, which she always had with her. She extracted the splinter as I wept bitter tears, not so much from pain, but because of our poverty, which I found incomprehensible, and because I thought our future was hopeless.

"I didn't know that my daughter was such a crybaby," observed Mother dispassionately (we were never a sentimental family). "Where do you get all that timidity? I never want to see another tear from you again!"

But I knew, I could sense, that things were far from easy for her either.

The days dragged by with tedious monotony. I was totally subservient to my mother, and she had forbidden me, most strictly, to leave our building or talk to anyone. Why? I did not dare ask. Her authority was absolute and not to be questioned.

In the morning I would tidy the room and then had to sit in it like a prisoner. This was a time of enforced, frustrating idleness. To alleviate the boredom, I would open the folders of my sheet music. Turning the pages, I could hear one melody after another in my head. Here was the last piece I had played for Professor Igumnov, Grieg's Sonata, with Igumnov's pencil notations indicating easier fingering for the left hand. No! This was more than I could bear. It was as though I were mentally wandering down the flowery paths of a lost paradise. I would slam my folders shut and open Mama's. But that was even worse, because then I would hear her voice, singing her favorite arias and romances. Here, too, there were pencil markings made by her for my benefit. They were scattered here and there throughout the technically complex accompaniment to Rachmaninov's romances, and consisted of one word only: "Learn!". That meant that I had made a mistake at that point. Of course, I had learned them long ago, knew them by heart, yet for some reason the flowing script of her peremptory command remained, as we had remained, alive. But why?

In the evening Mother would bring me her dinner, a piece of dried fish and two spoonfuls of cold porridge without butter in a metal cup. This was my one and only meal for the day. Of course, it was insufficient, but even worse, it was somehow shameful and humiliating. Born into luxury, accustomed to hearing about our wealth from all sides, surrounded by a large number of courteous and efficient servants, I did not, for some reason, have those traits so frequently ascribed to our privileged class. Neither I, my brother, nor any of my contemporaries ever felt that the world owed us a living, a regrettable characteristic I was to encounter later, and still do, among our young people today.

So when my mother returned from her first day at work and brought me her portion, I felt as though I had been slapped in the face. But I ate Mama's food. I choked as I ate it, despising myself. I ate it because I was constantly hungry.

Two weeks later, Mother came home in a state of some turmoil. Her job had been changed. There was a vacancy for a supervisor in the dining hall, and when it was learned that she could both read and write, the job went to her. The duties of cook were assumed by a tall, strapping, broad-shouldered, black-haired woman called Pelageya, whose regal bearing always put me in mind of the sister of Tsar Peter I, Princess Sophia.

It was not only Mama's literacy, but the unexpected executive ability she showed that was in demand. As far as anything else was concerned, though, there was no change. Her work place remained the same. She could not leave the cooking pots, but had to do her share of preparing breakfast, lunch, and dinner for the night-shift workers. I hardly saw her. Her whole life seemed to revolve around improving the meals and trying to introduce some variety into the menus. I began to think that she had found her true vocation in life.

I recalled an incident which occurred once on our favorite estate near Moscow, Petrovskoye. It is hard to imagine a more beautiful and magical place. The architect Tikhomirov called it a unique example of country estate architecture and published five photographs of it, including the floor plans.

The estate park was laid out on rising ground, so its twenty-seven hectares were always bathed in sunlight. The park was bisected by a broad avenue, just like the one on our Poltava estate, and lined with statues brought by the Meshcherskys from Florence and Rome. At the end of the avenue, a huge statue of Apollo stood on a rise: the greenish-black copper torso of the Greek god stood out in bold relief against a background of white lilies, which were planted around the statue's pedestal.

The right side of the park was laid out in formal French style, its avenues running at right angles to each other and lined with centuries-old linden trees whose blossoms scented the air with a heady aroma. The left side of the park, or "the wilderness" as it was called, was crisscrossed by mysterious paths and unexpected avenues with comfortable benches. The wilderness was really like a genuine wood: it had a small ravine overgrown with raspberry canes, and a spring of clear water. Further up, above the lip of the ravine, there were badger dens among the thick growth of firs. A small tributary of the Desna River ran at the foot of the rise on which the statue of Apollo stood. The banks of this stream were lined with weeping willows; nightingales sang at night in the undergrowth, and a place for bathing lay hidden around a bend.

Petrovskoye was so sunny and magnificent that every day spent there was an untold joy.

Not for nothing was Petrovskoye called unique. In the center of the estate, there was a white stone palace, which was decorated with sixteen large columns and eight smaller ones on its four porticoes. The building was surmounted by a dome covered with white copper, which shone blindingly both in summer and winter. Two broad, fan-shaped stairways led to the main doors, which were guarded by figures of sphinxes and roaring lions with paws upraised.

The palace was for the holding of balls and large receptions. There was a ballroom on the ground floor, with a large balcony above for the orchestra. The rooms adjacent to the ballroom contained the Meshchersky family museum and archives. For us children, the most fascinating exhibits in the museum were a mammoth's tusk, which had been found long ago on the spot where the palace was built, and a small bronze sculpture of the foot of a gypsy named Nastya, resting on a burgundy velvet cushion under a glass cover. Our father's brother, Ivan Vasilyevich Meshchersky, had fallen madly in love with Nastya, bought her from her tribe, and married her. Because of this, he had to leave the Household Cavalry regiment in which he served.

The museum also contained many weapons, bestowed on the Meshcherskys for military valor, and numerous medals. The Meshchersky archives were valuable not only for their wealth of ancient documents and manuscripts, but for the fascinating correspondence between the Meshcherskys and the Karamzins, our close relatives. My father's uncle, Pyotr Vasilyevich Meshchersky, was married to the daughter of the famous historian Nikolai Karamzin. She was the very same Ekaterina Nikolayevna Meshcherskaya to whom Pushkin dedicated his poem "Akathistos." She was a great friend of the poet and was later to write a moving description of his funeral. The archives also contained several letters written to my father by the poet Mikhail Lermontov, and a manuscript with his poem "Tell Me, O Branch of Palestine . . ." written in Lermontov's own hand. On one side of the sheet, Lermontov sketched a palm branch, as was his custom. The ink had faded to a light brown. . . .

The rooms of the palace were decorated by blue majolica

hearths and matching vases. Our hearth was so huge that a dancing couple could fit into it. An enormous spit was mounted in this hearth, used for roasting wild boar and moose in times gone by. There were still traces of soot around the chimney from those days when the sound of the hunting horn would summon the royal hunt.

The next floor of the palace housed an auditorium with a large stage. During the summer that I remember, a great number of guests passed through the palace: one of them was the famous tenor Leonid Vitalyevich Sobinov, who had been a fellow student of Mama's. He sang for us. There was also Konstantin Nikolayevich Igumnov, who as I have mentioned visited us several times during a concert season in Moscow, and the actress Maria Zankovetskaya, a friend of my mother's, who played some of her acclaimed scenes for us.

All our guests were enthralled by our chef-pastrycook. He had been employed in the tsar's kitchens in Petersburg, but was dismissed for excessive drinking or, as some maintained, for unruliness. In our employ, however, he worked with dedication and behaved impeccably.

Every day dinner was awaited with pleasurable anticipation, especially the dessert course. And nobody was ever disappointed. Lo and behold, ice cream would be served under a delicate canopy of "Venus hair," a fragile filigree veil of spun sugar, gathered together by a caramel comb and studded with "gems" of multicolored candied fruits, or a tray bearing a flambé liqueur-soaked pudding. On one occasion, I remember, dessert consisted of a vase made out of colored confectionery, filled with a "sea" of chocolate cream, on whose waves rode small biscuit gondolas crewed by little chocolate negroes. In short, out chef won everyone's admiration and completely conquered my heart, little sweet tooth that I was.

Again and again, I racked my brains, trying to think up some way of rewarding him for his efforts. At first I considered smashing my money box and asking someone to give him all my savings. On second thought, though, that seemed too pedestrian. I was an incurable romantic and idealist even then, and material rewards seemed somehow paltry. Money? How common! I could not possibly risk offending his sensibilities like that.

Then I thought of the most magnificent thing in the world— my mother. Every child thinks his mother is beautiful, and I had more reason than most: was not my mother's beauty cause for continual comment? So I decided that I must reward the chef in Mama's name, something that was bound to make him happy for the rest of his life. All that remained was to work out the practical details, but none of the schemes that came to mind had that ring of success about them.

It was midsummer. The feast day of St. Olga drew near, and a large dinner was planned to celebrate my Aunt Olga's nameday. For dessert on that day, we had my favorite— meringue. It was crisp on the outside, deliciously chewy on the inside, and smelled mouth-wateringly of vanilla. After dinner was over, I skipped out on to the terrace, brimming over with gratitude toward the chef. Then suddenly—inspiration! Three perfect dark red roses lay on the balustrade. They must have been left there by Aunt Talya, who liked to wear live flowers in her dark hair. Roses! Roses and Mama seemed to go together naturally. A wild scheme hatched in my mind in a flash. Snatching up the roses, I bolted some distance along the path which ran between the main building and the service quarters. Hurriedly, I pulled off the bracelet which had been a present from my godmother, Alexandra Miloradovna: it was an intricately engraved gold band with a large Persian turquoise set into it. I regarded this bracelet as my good luck charm and always wore it, but that could not be a consideration if it would make the chef happy.

One of the footmen, fair-haired Nikolai, came down the path, but I let him pass because I didn't trust him. He was too greedy for my purpose. A few more people came by, but I did not feel that any of them were sufficiently trustworthy, either.

Finally I saw Mikitka, as everyone called him, walking down the path toward me. He was good-natured and not too bright, and was employed to clean the lamps.

"Mikitushka, could you please give these roses and bracelet to the chef and tell him that they are from Princess Meshcher-skaya *herself*?" I asked, deliberately stressing the last word.

Then, my mission discharged, I ran off to the croquet lawn with a light heart. I had done my best. Loving my mother and considering her to be the epitome of perfection, I was blithely certain that I had made the chef the happiest man on earth by what I saw as a small, innocent deception. Little did I dream what a drama was precipitated shortly thereafter by my action.

All the negative impulses and passions the chef had been suppressing by throwing himself wholeheartedly into his work erupted like a volcano. When he received the three roses and gold bracelet, allegedly from "the princess herself," he lost his head completely. Young blood and pride combined placed their own interpretation on this gesture. He took it as a sign of Mama's special favor and, dazzled by the prospect it seemed to imply, went right off the rails, as the saying goes. He decided that a radical change of his lot was imminent and, anticipating a brilliant future, lost no time in getting roaring drunk. He then tore off his chef's hat and apron and flung them into the lake under the bemused stare of all the other servants. Both these stiffly starched marks of his office bellied up and floated on the surface. He thrust one of the roses into his buttonhole and, waving the other two in the air and bellowing a rendition of a song about "Vanka the doorman and the young princess," set off to force his way into Mama's presence.

"She's waiting for me!" he yelled, throwing punches at any-one who tried to restrain him. Particularly offensive were the double entendres in his song about Vanka the doorman which referred to some secret "known only to the featherbed and the young princess." The servants, who finally managed to over-power him, could see no reason for this sudden fit of seeming madness. He struggled so furiously that they had to resort to tying him up. As they did so, a child's gold bracelet fell out of his pocket.

Efforts began to clarify the mystery. Everyone knew that the bracelet was mine, but in any case I had no intention of trying to wriggle out of the situation. I was absolutely stunned by what had happened, but I understood quite clearly that ultimately I was to blame. What was most upsetting was that I was given no chance to explain my motives. Oh well, I was already sufficiently accustomed to the hardheartedness of adults.

I was punished by a whole week's confinement to my room, where I had to sit with the blinds drawn and without any reading matter at all except for the Bible that lay on my desk. My meals were served not only minus dessert, but also without any white bread. I was supposed to spend the week pondering my misdemeanor.

When I was finally "released," I learned that my beloved chestnut pony, Amy, had been given away to a zoo as an added punishment.

Vyacheslav, true to form, was curt and pithy in his condemnation. "Who do you think you are, Madame Pompadour or something? Giving your bracelet as a keepsake, indeed! I-di-ot!" He spat meaningfully to stress his contempt.

The chef was dismissed on the spot, but I was terribly upset to learn that they had taken my bracelet away from him. When I saw it in my mother's hands, I burst into tears and was even glad that she gave it away, then and there, to another girl, the daughter of our seamstress.

So in the end my good intentions brought immense grief to someone I had never seen, but wished to make happy.

5
Making Music,
Earning My Keep

$\mathcal{T}$he waterworks operated around the clock, so the dining hall had to work twenty-four hours a day, too. It seemed as though Mama clung to this fact. Frequently she would not return home for the night, but would drop around for an occasional few hours of sleep during the day when exhaustion finally caught up with her.

I did not blame her for this. It must have been difficult for her to lie with me on the bare floor and even to see me. Indeed, there were times when I felt she would have preferred that I did not exist at all. Very often she would not even look at me. But at work, surrounded by people, she could escape into her duties.

Mother was a woman of immense fortitude; moreover, she had been an actress, albeit in her youth. In our new life—a life she had chosen voluntarily in accordance with her convictions—she always managed to seem calm, but it was not an easy role to sustain.

Once I saw her coming toward our building and rushed to open the door, but after one glimpse of her I pulled it to quickly and quietly, watching her through a small crack. She came up the stairs like a sleepwalker, staring blankly ahead. It was almost as though she were in some kind of trance. What pictures were in her mind's eye, what was she remembering in those moments? Closing the door, I retreated to the far side of the room, my heart beating like a trip-hammer. I felt as though I had committed some gross discourtesy, spied upon something not intended for my eyes.

A few moments later Mama came in, smiling, and asked me some question or other. We began to talk about something mundane and innocuous. But watching her covertly, with a new and heightened awareness, I saw the dark rings under her eyes and traces of gray in her hair.

And on top of all her cares, this poor woman had to provide for me as well. Sitting in our room in enforced solitude and contemplating my pointless and humiliating existence, I became increasingly convinced that Mother could be wrong. What right did she have to reduce me to the status of a mute slave and parasite? I began to notice the strange way people looked at me when I went with our kettle for hot water. Those looks were a mixture of pity and curiosity, but pity was uppermost. I caught snatches of phrases here and there and realized that I was generally considered to be either abnormal or somehow deficient. "That's why she's afraid of people, that's why she stays shut up in their room . . ." This was the last straw. I seethed with rebellion and, in particular, rebellion against my own mother.

"I can't go on like this," I whispered to myself. "I've got to do something!" The question was, what?

One bright day in late autumn, when Mother had been sent to Moscow about some inventory or other, I walked out of our building, full of resolve, even though I had no clear idea about whom to approach. I stopped for a moment, breathing deeply of the cold air, redolent of the smell of fallen leaves. Through the bare branches of the trees which bordered Rublevo's streets, I saw a yard full of children, and the large schoolhouse. I could hear the children's happy voices, laughter, shouts. It must be the long break, I thought, that's why they're all outside.

With sudden and painful intensity, I wanted to join them. I wanted to laugh too, to run and play, sit behind a desk, see an open exercise book before me, take up a pen . . . I could almost smell the familiar odor of ink, but then sternly suppressed such unnecessary feelings and recollections.

With quickening pace, I headed for the school. As I approached, I saw an elderly man with long, gray whiskers standing on the school porch. He was watching me attentively, inquiringly.

"Good day," I ventured.

The old teacher acknowledged my greeting with a nod and continued to look at me in that same interrogative manner.

"Do you need anyone to sweep the floors, wash out dusters and inkwells, anything like that? I'm willing to do that sort of work in exchange for meals," I babbled. My heart sank as I saw his face darken with displeasure.

"Where are you from?" he demanded. "Any why haven't you been here before today?"

"I'm the cook's daughter," I managed weakly. "We came up from Moscow."

"So what? Why haven't you been here yet? Don't you know that the school year has already started? Where were you at school up until now?" he persisted.

"I didn't go to school anywhere," I lied, blushing furiously. "And I'm never going to go to school anywhere. I've come to find out about work!" I returned, feeling that I had managed to answer all his questions.

"Oho, it's like that, is it?" He adjusted his spectacles. "Who are you? Are you lazy or just plain stupid?" he went on angrily. "You can find the right job for yourself when you grow up, but in the meantime go home and think about the silliness of what you have just said. When you make up your mind to study, come back here, but until that time, stay away. . . . Now that I think of it, I have seen you before—you're always going back and forth with a kettle. You tell your mother that I want to have a word with her. Do you hear that? Clean the school . . . ! What next?!"

Turning on my heel, I hurried away without a backward glance. I could feel his eyes boring into my back. Of course, he meant well and could hardly have reacted to my question in any other way.

The failure of my initiative was a bitter pill to swallow. I spent the rest of that day holed up in our room and, for the first time, refused to go out for hot water when Mama returned from Moscow.

"What do you mean, you won't go?" asked Mama in some surprise.

"I've got a headache," I muttered.

She reached out automatically and touched my forehead, but, having satisfied herself that I was not running a temperature, said no more.

The next day I set off for the school again. The first time I had gone by guesswork and had encountered the senior master (he was also the mathematics teacher) of the senior school. This time I hoped to catch one of the schoolmistresses. There were many of them; they were all young, and I thought they would be more sympathetic to my request. I was wrong. The result in the junior school was identical. I stood in the middle of the large staff room, in a state of some confusion.

"We have no jobs for adolescents. They're all studying, and those of your age are in the senior school."

This response came from a teacher who sat at a table, sorting through a large pile of exercise books. Her tone brooked no argument, and the somewhat exaggerated attention she was paying to the books in front of her showed clearly that my case was hopeless.

"I'm sorry," I said quietly and went to the door with dragging steps.

I passed colorful maps pinned up on the wall, drawings. . . . Finished! You're finished! echoed inside me. I passed large windows with broad sills covered with potted plants, bright geraniums, waxy begonias. There were lots of small pots with cacti and a lemon tree in a tub. Everything was clean, bright, and sunny, growing with the same cheerful abandon as the laughing children out in the yard. But there was no place here for me. . . . Then I noticed a piano, which I had not seen in my agitation when I entered the staff room. Sheet music was scattered on its black, polished surface. I stopped in my tracks. Here was something I loved and knew, but I did not even dare stretch out my hand and touch the sheets of notes. All I could do was crane my neck for a glimpse of the names of the pieces.

"Are you fond of music?" I heard the teacher's voice behind me.

I nodded mutely.

"Do you play the piano, by any chance?"

I nodded again, still unable to say a word. Her chair scraped back and she walked over to me.

"Sit down and play something." She opened the instrument and nodded encouragingly at the keyboard.

I sat down and began to play the first thing that came into my head: Beethoven's *Three Contradances*. Seeing her smile of approval, I broke off and launched into Grieg's *Wedding Procession*.

"We need someone like you desperately!" exclaimed the teacher. "Can you pick up melodies by ear? 'The Internationale,' for instance?"

Trying not to make any mistakes, I began to pick out the tune of this oft-heard song.

"That's too low a key," commented the teacher. "Take it a bit higher, but not above high fa."

We became quite carried away, searching for a suitable key for group singing. We both sang, too, and for a little while I even forgot why I had come here. Finally, the teacher broke off our session and gave me a quick hug.

"You're going to teach singing," she told me. "Every day, you'll eat with us—for the time being, anyway—and then we'll see. And now tell me honestly: why don't you want to study?" She took me firmly by the shoulders and looked searchingly into my eyes.

"To tell the truth," I replied, looking back at her unflinchingly, "I cannot give you an answer to your question. I don't want to lie to you. I can never study again, but I do have to work. Do you understand?"

She released me immediately and returned to her desk. Now she looked at me with real understanding and, as though I had not spoken, asked, "Is it your mother who's working in the dining hall?"

"Yes."

"You've come from Moscow?"

"Yes . . ."

She was silent for a few moments, obviously turning something over in her mind.

"Right! I'll see what I can sort out for you at the school council. I think we'll come up with some solution. We really do need you. Later on we might be able to get you a teaching post. Unofficially, of course, if it works . . ." Then, as if fearing that she had said too much, she hurried on. "Today, after four o'clock when school's over, come here and we'll choose a few songs for you. We'll have to see whether you can manage. We'll sing "Bravely Comrades, All in Step," "We Are the Smiths," and "Hostile Tempests." I'll help you prepare for the first lesson."

Alexandra Nikolayevna Ivakina was the name of this kind young woman, whom I have never forgotten. She had a slightly retroussé nose, thick ash-blonde hair, and large, very dark, brown eyes. Her voice was a rich, delightful contralto, and I was to accompany her many times in the future at concerts in Rublevo. She sang Lyubava's aria from *Sadko*, Lel's pieces from

Snowdrop, and classical romances. I don't know what she thought of my mother and myself, but none of the teachers ever asked me anything again or urged me to become a pupil at the school.

On the evening of that fateful day I was not at home when Mama returned, bringing me her food as usual. The room was empty, and I only appeared around nine o'clock. Mother greeted me with a look that would have made my blood run cold in the past. But this time I was beyond fear of any kind and flung my arms around her neck, tongue tripping over my words as I blurted out my triumph.

"So you dared to disobey me after all!" said Mother in frigid tones, pulling out of my embrace. "You dared go against my will?!"

"Yes! And I'll do so every time you're wrong!" I retorted, stung, but not quite believing it was my voice saying those words.

"I can be *wrong?*" repeated Mother slowly. "Is that what you said?" Her face paled with anger.

"Yes!" I affirmed defiantly and far too loudly, as though it were not I, but someone else speaking. Lowering my voice, I continued more reasonably. "Please don't be angry with me! You still think I'm a small child, but I see everything, everything! Including your suffering! You must understand that I've got to earn my own keep!"

She looked at me in surprise, then dropped her eyes. When she raised them again, they were bright with tears. How I longed to throw my arms around her again! But I quashed the impulse and, pretending that I had noticed nothing, turned away. . . .

It is impossible to describe how wonderful my life became after that. I threw myself into my work with the same joy with which someone dying from heat would throw himself into the cool waters of a deep river. No longer did every new day stretch before me like an arid wasteland. I was taken on for a month's trial, but that entitled me to regular meals. These consisted of a very thin wheaten soup and frostbitten potatoes, but they were potatoes, nonetheless. The food was served hot and seemed an incredible luxury in those hungry years. More than anything, I valued my small piece of grayish, half-baked bread, which I earned with my own labor. The fare was standard issue for all the workers, and it was mine, too. It filled my heart with joy and pride, and I no longer feared the future. There was work enough, that I knew. I also knew something else: I was needed!

However, my first day at work also brought my first difficulties. As if by some conspiracy, the children at the school refused to see me as a teacher, but treated me as an equal. They did not want to obey me, and some of them set out to make nuisances of themselves. This applied mainly to the boys from the senior classes, whose voices were just beginning to sound adult and whose first fluffy whiskers were only beginning to sprout.

At choir classes, when Alexandra Nikolayevna was present and led the singing with her rich contralto, all would be well. But when it came to lessons on theory, I was left to conduct the class on my own, and all hell would break loose. They were particularly fond of making fun of my perpetually red cheeks (possibly a symptom of my heart trouble) and my curly hair, which no brush could tame, try as I might.

"Katerina's come to class all rouged up!" they would chant in unison. "And she's done up her hair in corkscrews!"

This would go on until I would leap up in fury (which was exactly what they wanted) and we would all head for the washroom, where I would wet my hair (making it curl all the more) and scrub my cheeks until they were redder than ever in a futile effort to prove my tormentors wrong.

It was not long before the other teachers realized what was happening, and they decided to help me. The senior master, the one I had encountered on my first visit to the school, began to sit in on the music theory lessons. I don't know why, but I never got over my fear of him. He really did frighten me: ever alert, looking sternly over the tops of his spectacles, enormous whiskers bristling, he sat through the lessons in silence. It seemed to me that those whiskers moved with a life of their own. The chalk slipped in my hand, the lines I drew on the board were crooked, and the notes came out lopsided. But you could hear a pin drop in that classroom from the beginning of the lesson to the end.

Despite such problems, my month's trial went well, and the school council referred my case to the Ministry of Education in Moscow. The chairman of the council traveled to Moscow to support the request himself. My appointment remained "casual." In this way, I became the singing teacher.

"Well, you're a teacher now," said Mother with a condescending smile. "So you'll have to behave accordingly. No more skipping across the yard when you go for hot water, no more jumping over puddles like a frisky goat. I'll give you some hairpins and show you how to put up your braids."

Passing through our first baptism by hard work, after the first arrests and the loss of family members, we were both still feeling our way and welcomed labor of any kind. It was only due to the shortage of people (I mean people who had a contribution to make, but were still undecided whether they should work for the Bolsheviks or wait for possible "better times" ahead) that my mother was able to become first a cook and then dining-hall supervisor and I, a green girl, a teacher.

Nowadays just about every child learns to sing or play an instrument, some professionally, others at home or at evening classes. At home they can listen to the radio, pick up the songs they like by ear, carry around transistor radios. But there was nothing like that in the far-off years of 1917 and 1918 in Rublevo. Yet the desire for music was there, and because of that I was swamped by the local youth when it became known that I could play the piano.

Not a single movie screening in Rublevo's well-appointed auditorium took place now without me. Films were still silent in those days and needed a piano accompaniment. Seated behind

the screen, I could watch the action and accompany every scene
with appropriate music. At first this did not work very well, and
I was afraid that I would be unable to cope. My first attempts
were not particularly successful. I made mistakes and occasionally broke off altogether. This would provide an immediate
storm of whistles and shouts from the public. "Hey, Katya!
Come on! Where's the music? Get going!"

I experienced the greatest difficulties with films starring
Douglas Fairbanks, Max Linder, and Charlie Chaplin. All these
movies needed a fast and furious accompaniment, far removed
from my classical repertoire.

After a while, however, I learned to accompany all the
stunts, tricks, and frantic car chases by playing technical etudes
very rapidly. After that, all went smoothly. Before the actual
screening of the movie, I would ask for a private preview, so
that I could select suitable music in advance. But this raised
another problem: I had to improvise links between the chosen
pieces, so that I could pass unnoticed from one to another. Actually, I did not do too badly. I even rather fancied some of my
own composition.

I was now surrounded by a crowd of my contemporaries
every time I took up my station behind the screen. They would
watch the movie and my piano playing with equal delight, for
in their eyes I was a real pianist. Deep inside I felt a little ashamed
of myself: what would my music professor have said if he heard
the musical potpourri of which I was both composer and
performer?

However, my prestige rose to giddy heights among the
youth of Rublevo. I even began to get romantic notes, worded
along such lines as: "Katya! Why don't you go out with anyone?
Will you go out with me?" or "Katya! Let's go walking together
near the filters. I've liked you for a long time." There was one
note in particular which I kept for my personal archives: "Katya!
I've fallen in love with you like a pig, and can't think of anything
else. Let's go dancing together. . . ."

My mother became very annoyed when I showed her these notes.

"We want none of that!" she exclaimed. "It's all your own fault, you know. You sing and dance far too much! Behave with a bit more decorum and remind them that you're a teacher. Anyway, you're far too young to go out with anyone. Hear me?"

I did go walking around the filters, though, when everyone was asleep and I went to meet Mother during a break in her round-the-clock shifts. It was a fascinating place, a large, flat expanse with round depressions where there were underground water filters. Some were closed, others rose above ground level. As I wandered among them, I would weave all sorts of fantasies. The snowy expanse around me would become some ancient Russian battlefield, and the covers of the filters shields of warriors fallen in battle. The sound of the wind became transformed into a symphony orchestra, and Ruslan's aria "Oh Field, Field, Who Has Strewn Thee with Dead Bones?" from Glinka's famous opera echoed in my head.

I also loved roaming Rublevo's snow-covered streets. The stark patterns of bare branches moved above my head against a background of clear winter sky, and I would imagine myself back in the park of Petrovskoye, that beloved bit of land where my short childhood had sped by.

When Mother was on night duty, I would occasionally indulge in a secret pleasure. Because of my leading role in club work, I was entrusted with a key to the club house. There was no time to play the piano during the day, so I would do so at night, letting myself into the empty building and locking the door behind me. I would then grope my way to the stage in the dark, light a small lamp, pull out the books of music from their storage place, and sit down and play.

The auditorium was dark, but I would pretend that it was ablaze with lights and packed with people. I would play piece after piece, losing all sense of time and place. I imagined that I was a renowned pianist, whose performance was greeted by thunderous applause. I was still very silly and fanciful in those days.

But life, real life with its attendant demands, tore me away from my girlish dreams. One had to sleep at night in order to have enough energy for the next day's tasks. And there was more than enough of those. I did not have a single free moment. It seemed as if everyone wanted to sing, and I had to accompany them all. All the school performances included music, too. Every time I accompanied a movie in the clubhouse, there was no question of going straight home afterward, because the audience would all want to dance. So I would play waltzes, Polish folk dances, pas d'Espagnes, polkas, endless Russian folk dances, and, of course, the fiery gypsy dances.

Living in Rublevo was an elderly German or Austrian man called Walter. After the First World War, he had remained in Russia for some reason, and he was an extremely gifted, self-taught violinist. Some of the Rublevo lads who could play the mandolin, the guitar, or the balalaika teamed up with him to form a band, but they lacked a leader, which is what I became when they asked me to play the piano for them. This band became a favorite not only of Rublevo but many surrounding villages.

However, not everything was trouble-free on our "cultural front," and I witnessed many very nasty incidents. The various functions at the Rublevo club were attended not only by locals but also by young people from nearby villages, Pavshina, Zakharkina, and others.

At that time, there was a great deal of illegal brewing of alcohol in the Moscow region, and young people would come for an evening out to Rublevo with bottles of this "hooch." All the bottles would be consumed secretly in record time. Movie shows or concerts were usually followed by dancing, during which all the boys naturally vied for the attention of the girls. Well primed with "hooch," the lads looked for excuses to pick quarrels with each other. The most common reason was jealousy, which provoked fights. And what fights! It would start with punches, and end up as a free-for-all in which switchblade knives replaced fists.

As more and more evening entertainments and dances were held at the club, this was where the young people spent all their free time. Many came from the surrounding area, bringing their instruments in the hope of joining the Rublevo band.

Of course, a piano is a piano, and work in the club without it would have been impossible. However, I cannot claim any particular credit in this instance, young and inexperienced as I was. My leader and mentor in singing classes at the school was Alexandra Nikolayevna, and in the work of the band all credit was due to Walter, the first and only fiddle in our band. It was thanks to these two people that I was able to gain some self-confidence, while the music acted as a bond that gradually diluted the earlier rivalry based on the attitudes that "our Rublevo girls are ours only, we're one crowd, and you're outsiders."

One might ask how was it that I, an adolescent, formerly a pupil of a closed school, could know anything about a string-instrument band? As it happens, by the time I was nine years old, I already played the balalaika a little in our own domestic orchestra. Artistic expression was considered very important in our family, and we had our own amateur theatre. We were all musical: Mama sang, my brother played the violin, and I, the piano. Once my brother and his friends organized a small string orchestra. He immediately sat me down to play the second balalaika. It was a huge instrument for a small child to handle, so it kept sliding off my lap. Seeing my difficulties, Vyacheslav decided to give me a little encouragement.

"Now stop puffing and panting," he said, encouragingly. "Chin up! You're the only girl here. That's an honor, you know, so be proud of it!"

Naturally, these words worked wonders for my morale, but they did nothing for my playing. The balalaika had three strings, each one thicker than the last. The accompaniment was not a difficult one, two or three chords only, but I couldn't seem to get them right, especially the changes.

"Why do I have such an idiot for a sister?" Vyacheslav would exclaim in exasperation, giving me an occasional surreptitious clip on the ear. "If you're so tone deaf, then watch me. I'll give you the sign when to change the chord!"

The thick, tough strings made my fingers sore and raised blisters on my skin.

"I can't play anymore," I whimpered. "My fingers hurt!"

"Worse things happen in war," Vyacheslav would respond in minatory accents, and give me another clip on the ear to galvanize my efforts. After a while I managed to grasp the basics and could anticipate the time to change cords by myself.

Later I went on to play the first balalaika and even the mandolin. After a while it became my responsibility to tune all the instruments before rehearsals or performances. I also learned a great deal from our domestic theater, which was one of the greatest interests of my childhood.

The theater . . . it was the favored form of entertainment not only for people of our class, but everyone. Plays were staged wherever possible—in old barns, half-finished buildings, park pavilions, and terraces of stately homes, to say nothing of specially built amateur theaters.

As I have already mentioned, our theater, with a seating capacity of two hundred people, was on the first floor of the palace. The wardrobe was in the basement; trunks upon trunks of costumes were stored there. These trunks were all unlocked with an intricate copper key. When it was inserted in a lock and turned, melodies reminiscent of music-box tunes would sound. One of the trunks contained old military uniforms, feathered tricorne hats, cavalry boots with enormous, comical spurs, rapiers, and swords. Other trunks held ancient, coquettish crinolines, lace, shawls, the gowns of long-dead ladies-in-waiting, many old ball dresses, and all kinds of fans, made from lace or feathers, or beautifully painted by the hands of artists.

As a small child, I yearned to get on the stage. How I envied the adults who performed plays, vaudevilles, charades! But there was never a part for me, and my brother would invariably nip my aspirations in the bud with a standard hardhearted response: "That's no place for your little nose!" And he would lightly flick the said nose with a careless finger. It didn't hurt physically, but it did hurt my pride. Pretending not to care, I would run off and hide in the wings, to listen to the participants practicing their lines, or would watch them rehearse.

And then, once, there was something for me to do, too! The play called for a small negro. My joy knew no bounds! But when I realized that they were going to blacken my face and hands and stick huge red lips made out of felt over my mouth, I burst into tears and refused.

However, the little negro was vital to the action. So they pulled one of Nanny's thick black stockings over my head and cut eyeholes in it, around which they sewed large white circles. Then they cut a hole for the mouth and attached those same red felt lips to it. I did not really mind this. My only complaint was that the stocking flattened my nose uncomfortably. Instead of blacking my hands, I wore a pair of Mama's black gloves.

Finally the magic hour arrived! The stage curtains whispered apart and the handsome sultan (Vyacheslav, of course), wearing a gem-encrusted turban, reclined majestically on a couch under a silken canopy. A crowd of newly acquired slave girls stood a little to the side. Every time the elderly vizier clapped his hands, two eunuchs would lead one of the new slaves forward. I stood by, fanning the sultan with a large fan on a long stick. Actually it was quite heavy. Every movement made the woolen stocking tickle my face, and my heavy breathing filled my nostrils with bits of fluff. Thinking to get rid of them, I breathed in deeply, and the result was just the opposite. I sneezed so violently that for a moment my feet left the ground. The rest was horrifically inevitable: the fan caught the silken canopy and it crashed to the ground, its tassels and beads clicking and swaying.

The slave girls squealed and scattered. One of them caught her tunic on something, and it tore in half, forcing her to make her escape half-naked, to the appreciative laughter of the audience.

Thus my sneeze utterly destroyed the scene depicting the beauties of the East and plunged me into deep disgrace. Nevertheless I continued to nurse my passion for the stage deep in my heart. The backstage smells, the sound of the opening curtain, the dark pit of the auditorium—all held me in thrall.

Then—oh, joy!—they thought of me on another occasion. The reason was that someone among the adults noticed how I used to love swinging on the maypole, and the higher, the better.

Rehearsals for a staging of Gogol's *Evenings on a Farm near Dikanka* were in progress, and in one scene they needed to have a witch sweep across the sky on a broomstick, while at the same time she lies without breathing on the grass in the body of the peerless Pannochka.

A metal crossbar was rigged up across the top of the stage, with a kind of metal basket attached to it. A large broom was thrust through it, so from the auditorium it looked as though I were sitting astride the broomstick, long black skirts flying. I wore an incredibly ugly witch's mask with a long, hooked nose and a black kerchief on my head, from which straggly wisps of white "hair" protruded to complete the picture. It was all highly effective. As I flew across the sky, I was first to squeal, then howl like a dog, and then squeal again. The rehearsals went without a hitch. I practically deafened all the actors with my keening and wailing, and they would block their ears, laughing, before rewarding me with applause. I felt very pleased with myself. But on the night of the premier, the stagehands were a little too zealous and shot my basket out much too forcefully. It literally flashed across the stage and fetched up with a crash in the wings. The only thing that saved me from serious injury was that the broomstick took the first impact and snapped with a sharp crack. My forehead was, however, cut and bleeding, and instead of witch's wails and howls, the theater resounded to the frightened yells and tears of a child.

That was the end of my theatrical career. Mama forbade me not only to hang around during rehearsals but also to attend any performances. My governess didn't let me out of her sight for one moment and accompanied me everywhere. I went around with a bandaged head for almost the whole of that summer, and it took a long time for the abrasions and contusions on my forehead to disappear.

Although my doomed theatrical appearances had long been forgotten, one person recalled them and even wanted to put me on the stage again. This was my brother's teacher of Greek, Stepan Melisari, and his close friend, Pannayotis Konzampopoulo, who had come over from Athens on a visit.

Youth always calls to youth. Melisari and Pannayotis, who often stopped by to visit the steward in his quarters, met and became friendly with the three so-called former criminals, about whom I shall tell more later. And these, in their turn, had become close friends with the steward's student sons.

I was always glad to see the early afternoon tea brought around because afterward my governess either read a novel while reclining in a hammock, wrote letters to her relatives, or went off to her room for a light nap. In the meantime, I would go for my riding lesson in the charge of our riding master, Smett. He was of medium height, gray-haired, and very kind, but strict in demanding effort and application. If Smett was busy with something else, I was allowed to take my toys and retreat to the farthest reaches of the park. It was here that I would frequently encounter Melisari, Pannayotis, and the other denizens of the steward's house. Usually they would call me over to join them and ask me to recite poetry to them. I knew a great many poems by heart and enjoyed reciting them. This was not as good as appearing on the stage, of course, but my imagination supplied the necessary props.

On one such occasion, Melisari said to me, "Don't fret. We shall fix up a stage appearance for you, and very soon."

I almost stopped breathing with excitement.

"But what will Mama say? And Vyacheslav? Who'll let me?"

"Everything will have to be done in secret," whispered Melisari conspiratorially. "Not a word to anyone! Total secrecy! We'll disguise you, and by the time anyone realizes who you are, it will be too late. You'll get more applause than Yermolayeva (a reigning actress of the time). We'll show all those who haven't appreciated you just how wrong they were. Chin up, Ginger Snap! We're all in this conspiracy now, so see that you don't spill the beans!"

Vanity was always my besetting sin. I was highly flattered by this offer. Adults knew all too well what bait to use to trap me: lust for glory turned my head, and I burned with one desire—to get revenge for Mama's strictness with me and to make a monkey out of my bossy brother.

I no longer hid my forbidden writing under the carpet in the playroom. I now stowed them away behind the books on my bookshelf. Pannayotis slipped me a page torn out of some anthology with Aleksei Pleshcheyev's poem "All Men Are Brothers" on it. I folded it four times and hid it behind my books.

After two or three more meetings with my fellow conspirators, I had the poem down pat. But then I realized something that could have unpleasant consequences for me. Virtually the entire front row in our palace theater consisted of "personal" chairs, and one of these, in the very center, was always reserved for Alexander Dmitriyevich Samarin, the marshal of Moscow nobility and a well-know government figure in tsarist Russia. This kindly old gentleman was universally respected and was a particular favorite among children. And I was supposed to point an accusing finger specifically at him during my recital of the

Plescheyev poem when I reached the words "Rich man! You wear luxurious clothes!" Then I was to shake my finger threateningly right under his nose. But that would mean insulting our friend, shaming him in front of the entire audience!

"I can't do that!" I whispered, despairingly. "I can't . . ."

Pannayotis ran a hand through his shock of dark hair and stared at me with his green, catlike eyes in disbelief.

"So we were mistaken in you after all! You're no actress! A real actress has no personal feelings, likes, or dislikes. She must transcend herself. You are supposed to be speaking as a poor ragamuffin, a beggar, about whom Plescheyev wrote this poem. Your family has been hounded into an early grave by cruel landowners. And this poor little boy is the only one left, without a roof over his head, with nowhere to go."

"But all the peasants are free now! And Alexander Dmitriyevich doesn't have any serfs!" I protested.

"But that's just it!" chimed in Melisari with a smile. "There's nothing like that these days. That's what the theater is for—it can re-create any epoch. If you're an actress, then you must forget about being Kitty Meshchersky and become a poor little beggar boy. And Samarin is not Samarin, either. There's nothing personal in it. He's the marshal of the nobility and represents the class of people whom this poor little beggar hates so much. That's all there is to it, you see? And it's up to you to convince the audience. This appearance of yours will show just how much real talent you have, understand? You just wait and see how everyone's going to applaud you!"

When the time came, my performance was rewarded with thunderous applause. The rafters rang with cries of "bravo" and "encore," and my heart swelled with pride until I though it would burst. Dimly, I saw Samarin's surprised and somewhat bewildered face; Vyacheslav, white with anger and biting his lip, always a giveaway sign of his vexation; my grandmother's shapely hand, fanning her flushed face too quickly with a lace fan. But these were only fleeting impressions. I was riding high on the wave of my success. Had I not always wished to be a boy? I was delighted that my braid had been tucked away out of sight under a large, faded cap with a cracked lacquered peak. On my feet I wore a dirty pair of peasant bast sandals and torn leggings, wound around with a piece of rope. When I tired of taking curtain calls, Melisari picked me up and carried me out to the front of the stage. He lifted me high in the air, turning my back to the audience, showing them a huge brown patch sewn onto the seat of my dark pants. The effect was tremendous, and the audience roared their appreciation. I must confess that I was rather put out by this, because I felt that the sight of that patch detracted from the dramatic content of my performance.

Then the intoxication of the moment began to recede and was replaced by the suspicion that serious punishment was about to follow. Strangely enough, however, it did not. There were two reasons for this: first, among the prominent guests at the palace at that time were the Gorchakovs from Moscow and the Meshcherskys from Petrograd, as well as Maria Zankovetskaya, the "Ukrainian Yermolayeva," who was playing a season in Moscow. Second, the strict rules of hospitality made it impossible for Mama to ask Pannayotis Konzampopoulo, the mastermind behind my performance, to leave. Not only was he a childhood friend of Melisari, but also the nephew of Archbishop Arseni, who lived in Athens and who had for many years been Father's confessor.

It was therefore thought expedient to treat my performance as a lighthearted prank perpetrated by thoughtless young people.

Vyacheslav remained diplomatically silent, punishing me with his unconcealed contempt, but once his anger did find expression. He encountered me in one of the far avenues of the park at a time when everyone usually took an afternoon rest. I was on my way to one of the pavilions with a book when he suddenly barred my path.

"Off to see your pals, are you? Going to practice reciting something else, no doubt?"

I stood before him in silence, expecting him to give me a customary clout.

"You stupid idiot!" he said, not laying a finger on me. "Those revolutionaries really used you, didn't they? Fine friends you've found . . ."

He turned away sharply and walked off with a rapid step, whistling a cavalry march.

6
Mama's Secret Gift

$\mathcal{M}$other had her own difficulties in her job as dining hall supervisor. None of her predecessors had lasted long, as most of them were local people from nearby villages who simply could not resist the temptation to "economize" on the workers' food. It would not be long before these supervisors would manage to acquire a calf, or a cow, or buy a whole separate cottage. Then an auditing commission would arrive without warning and uncover embezzlement of funds and shortages of provisions. The guilty parties would be fired, and the Rublevo dining room would be without a supervisor again. My mother threw herself into her new work heart and soul. She also discovered a real flair for cooking, even with the limited food supplies of those years. It was not long before there was a marked improvement in all the meals because products that had been previously thrown out or wasted were now used rationally. So it was possible, even in those lean times, to start deducting less from the workers' pay toward their meals, and for this they were duly grateful. Very often people would come up to Mother after they finished eating, shake her hand and thank her.

The reason for her success was plain: she was honest. And then, suddenly, Mother began to get threatening anonymous letters. These letters advised her to "clear out before it's too late," to "go back to where she'd come from," otherwise she would "get a knife in her ribs." Mother said nothing about these letters, but I would find them myself, pushed under our door. I pretended that I didn't care about them either, even though I saw Mama's anxiety. However, she was no coward and continued to go out at night across the fields to the dining hall to check out the meals of the night shift. I never found out how she managed to deal with her unnamed enemies. I suspect that the workers themselves helped her, because they held her in high regard.

Sunday was a hard day for both of us. As we got our meals at work, Sunday meant no food. Therefore I agreed to give music lessons to the two children of a local engineer. They paid for these lessons with milk, because they owned a cow. Then I took on another pupil, who paid in potatoes. This meant that we could eat our fill, and Mother used to laugh, saying that on Sundays she was my dependent. Even though this was a joke, it still contained a grain of truth, and this made me very proud and happy.

By tacit mutual consent, we both avoided contact with the Rublevo intelligentsia. Even at school I never talked about anything unrelated to work with any of the teachers, though I would frequently catch them looking, watching me with thoughtful interest. Mother and I gravitated to the workers and felt ourselves much more at home and at ease among them.

It was only then that I came into direct contact with those people from whom I had been totally cut off by the wall of my social origins. In my childhood, the peasants were just crowds who came, singing, up the road leading to our estate. They would come bearing the first sheaf of wheat or celebrating some church feast day. Trestle tables covered with food would be set out for them on the lawns in front of the palace. They would be given money, and sometimes a barrel of wine would be brought up for them from the cellars.

On the estate near Moscow we saw more of them. On frosty days during the Christmas holidays, we would cover several miles on skis and then make a stop in some village or other, going into any house to wax our skis. We would be given a warm welcome. A copper samovar would be put on to boil, and carefully cleaned eggs were often placed inside it to cook. We would spread freshly churned butter on the fragrant home-baked bread and dip into saucers full of aromatic, dark gold honey.

It may not sound very credible for me to claim that my mother enjoyed excellent relations with the peasantry, even though I, her daughter, who was to continue such relations, could write a whole book of examples about the deep and mutual affection and respect that existed in our past with the common people. Throughout my whole life I have benefited from their many kindnesses and help.

Instead, I shall limit myself to just several facts that can be checked. The peasants paid our steward a certain fee for the right to water their stock on a stretch of our land. Once they held a council and came to see my mother, asking her to let them purchase that piece of land outright.

"You can have it without paying a penny," said Mother, and immediately wrote out a deed of gift.

She was also the only one in our district to endow schools, which made it possible for peasant children to continue their education for another four years on top of the four years provided by the church-funded parochial schools. She helped teachers who had large families by giving them a cow.

In Petrovskoye, there were two magnificent red brick buildings dating from the time of the Demidovs. (They were the former owners of Petrovskoye, descendants of the blacksmith Demidov, and neighbors of the Meshcherskys, who at that time owned the Pokrovskoye estate. When one of the Meshcherskys married one of the Demidov ladies, the two estates became one.) These two buildings were used as succession houses, in which Gabikosta, a gardener specially brought over from Greece, raised all manner of exotic fruits. His speciality was a particular strain of pink peaches, with which the Meshcherskys liked to surprise their guests.

At that time there were no fast electric trains doing the Kiev run, there was only one narrow-gauge track, which needed constant repairs, along which ran a small "Puffing Billy," which had to stop at each set of points and wait for oncoming trains to pass through. According to the timetable, this small train was supposed to cover a distance of forty-five versts in two hours, but in fact it was invariably at least an hour late. Because of this, the landowners in the area, including us, preferred to drive their guests in a carriage to Golitsino, where there was much better and more frequent service along the Alexandrovskaya (now the Belorussian) railway line.

Apart from a pharmacy, there were no shops of any kind either in Pokrovskoye or Petrovskoye, and the peasants did not have either the time or the money to travel to Moscow.

"It won't kill us to manage without pink peaches," decided Mother. She paid off Gabikosta, financed his return to sunny Greece, and set about refurbishing the succession houses into excellent shops, which sold a wide variety of goods and were called "consumer stores" by the peasants. Mother deeded both buildings and the land they stood on to the peasants. At the beginning of the Revolution, one of these buildings became the headquarters of the first regional executive committee.

From the first days of the Revolution and in the succeeding years, none of the peasants lifted a finger against us. On the contrary, when the famine set in, some of the peasants would seek us out in Moscow and bring us milk, bread, or even a piece of meat. The famine was really severe, and this food was given to us out of the little the peasants had for their own families.

But history is history, and even if Mother was something of an exception to the rule, we had ample opportunity to witness the vengeance wreaked by the peasantry on their former oppressors. The latter, sensing the imminent reckoning which could cost them their lives, tried to hide, to flee to some far-off corner of our immense country where they were unknown, or if worst came to the worst to escape abroad, to foreign lands.

I revere my mother's memory and have always been grateful to her for her honest and irreproachable life, which make it possible for me to remain in the old country without having to fear any unwelcome encounters from the past and to be able to look the world in the eye without flinching.

Yet then, in 1917–18, the anger of the people raged like a storm. They had overthrown the tsarist autocracy, were gradually settling their scores with the aristocracy, and were bound to destroy us, too, sooner or later. That was my conviction on the day of our arrival in Rublevo. But everything worked out quite differently. As soon as Mother and I became fully immersed in our work, we found ourselves at the very heart of the Rublevo family of workers. Hands of friendship were extended to us on all sides, and we felt and appreciated their support.

The working people began to drop in on us from the very beginning, on this or that matter of business. Of course they saw the conditions in which we lived, and assistance was not long in coming. We locked our room as a matter of course, but everyone knew that the key lay on one of the radiators, so anyone at all could enter our room at any time if they wanted. Once we came home to find two clean, sackcloth mattresses filled with sweet-smelling straw in our room. A little later, two flannel sheets appeared just as anonymously and mysteriously, then two small feather pillows, and finally two patchwork blankets of excellent quality and workmanship. All our efforts to establish who our benefactors were met only with headshakes and smiles. Not knowing whom to thank specifically, we thanked everyone, and I am sure that we were right to do so, for they all helped us when and how they could.

"What's that metal box you've got there in the corner?" someone once asked Mama.

"All that we have left in the world," she answered simply.

"In that case, you should hide it," was the sage advice. "None of our Rublevo folk'll touch it, but you get all sorts coming from around the district. Anything can happen. It's not all that private here, after all . . ."

Whenever Mother made a decision, she would implement it immediately. And that was how she acted then.

In order to understand and appreciate the rest of this story, one must bear in mind the psychological climate of that time, when nothing had any worth, when there was nobody to buy anything and many millionaires starved to death with a hoard of jewelry under their pillows, as well as gold ten-ruble coins with Nicholas II's image on them. The reader must also try to understand my mother's psychology, the psychology of a woman who had lost her family, the roof over her head, and who was therefore not inclined to waste much thought on the box of valuables which had come into her possession quite unexpectedly. We only found out the true value of its contents when, just as unexpectedly, we found ourselves in Moscow again.

Serving the workers' meals, my mother could see all their faces through the serving hatches. Her attention was caught by the face of an elderly, serious-looking man with deep-set, honest gray eyes. Mama asked him if he could come around to our room that evening. Everyone knew us, and he came that very day.

"I have a favor to ask of you," said Mama. "We don't really know anyone here. My daughter and I came from Moscow, where we became homeless, and all our worldly goods are inside this case. May I ask you, as a local resident, to take it for safe-keeping?"

"What's in it?" he asked, quite understandably.

Instead of answering, Mother took the key, opened the case, and showed him the contents.

"Where did you get that from?" he asked in amazement. "How did you come by it? And is it all real?"

"Here's the receipt I was given when the bank requisitioned the contents of our safe. I was astonished myself to get all this, but colored precious stones were not subject to requisition. Please have a look at this paper—it has all the necessary details, my surname, my name, and patronymic . . ."

"Where could I put it?" said the man, as though thinking aloud. "Hide it, perhaps? I really don't know."

"Wherever you think best. But perhaps I should ask someone else?"

"No, never mind, you'd better let me take it," he said, still looking thoughtful. Then suddenly he smiled. "Tell me, why did you choose me?"

"I didn't really choose," said Mother frankly. "It was just some impulse, I can't really explain. In any case, I was advised to put it somewhere safe . . ." She broke off awkwardly.

"Oh, my!" he said, looking at Mother with a mixture of pity and surprise. "You'd think that you'd have a bit of worldly wisdom at your age, but you're helpless as a small child! Lots of us here have gardens, apple trees, cherries. In autumn we can get hordes of gypsies coming through, offering to tell fortunes and at the same time stealing everything that's not nailed down . . . washing that's hanging out to dry, that sort of thing. And they sneak into the living quarters quite often, too . . . However," he interrupted himself and stretched out a hand to clasp Mother's, "let's get acquainted. My name's Ivan Ivanovich, and I live in the fourth concrete house along the avenue leading to the school."

Without further ado, he scooped up our case and went away.

The days flashed by. Mother and I were totally engrossed in our jobs. The carefully concealed agitation I had sensed in

Mother when we first came to Rublevo had disappeared. In her free time she would sit in our room, darning stockings and mending our few items of clothing.

We no longer spent long sleepless hours at night, tortured by recollections of the trials of the recent past; when we both knew that the other was awake; when I literally had to bit my tongue and bend my willpower to the limit not to break the silence, not to start talking, or crying, or complaining.

We were supported and comforted by the kindness and goodwill we encountered among the people of Rublevo. The knowledge that we were needed, that we worked as hard as everyone else, lent us confidence and enabled us to sleep soundly and greet every new day with pleasurable anticipation. There was no more oppressive feeling of loneliness and isolation. We lived and worked as members of a new and close-knit family.

It was not until later that I was able to appreciate what was happening to us in those days. Without realizing it ourselves, the fact that we were usefully employed changed us, and the people around us began to treat us differently. The young people of Rublevo became my close friends. I shall never forget Mefodi Firsayev, with his brilliant green eyes, black-haired Petro Konstantinov, Shura Melnikov, who was always in some scrape or other, Misha Makarov, who played first mandolin in our band. I could never forget Seryozha Eremin, our blue-eyed, fair-haired carpenter, either. How I wept when I accidentally broke the washbasin in our room! He came immediately, put in a new one, and convinced me that he had simply written off the one I had broken. I later found out by chance that he paid for the new one out of his own pocket. As for the marvelous girls in Rublevo, they deserve to be written about separately.

On some school days, I would be sent to Moscow. I hated making these trips. At that time there was no direct communication link between Moscow and Rublevo. The only way to get from one place to the other was either to go on the truck which shuttled back and forth or to catch the train which ran on the small branch line between Rublevo and Nemchinov Post and change there to an ordinary passenger train into Moscow. Traveling in the open truck in winter wearing a very light coat—the only one I possessed—was out of the question, so I would catch the train.

To catch the seven o'clock morning service meant getting up and slogging across windy fields while it was still dark. There, on a narrow, almost toylike track, a local lad nicknamed "Engine Volodya" would bring up his train. It consisted of a small steam engine with an enormously high smokestack and two ancient freight cars that were so dilapidated you could see all the passing scenery through the cracks in their walls. The wind swept through the carriages virtually unimpeded.

After ploughing knee-deep through snowdrifts in my low leather shoes, frozen to the bone, I would arrive in my flimsy coat at the point where Volodya took on passengers and clamber into one of the carriages. In the meantime Engine Volodya, a squat, short-armed youth, would flash the whites of his eyes in his soot-begrimed face, jump up and down to keep warm, and exhort the passengers scrambling onto the already moving train: "Come on. Step lively, now! Hurry up, no delays!"

I would arrive in Moscow, which I had left with such grief, but now it seemed a gloomy, alien place. There were no trams running, the sidewalks were piled high with snow, and endless crowds of pedestrians clutching bundles or with sacks on their backs moved listlessly along the streets. People went out into the countryside in search of bread and returned to Moscow with typhus. The city was in the grip of an epidemic. The sick lay in their thousands in unheated rooms lit by smoking oil lamps with no water coming through the frozen pipes.

After a day of trekking through numerous offices, I would finally repair to the Alexandrovsky railway terminal, into the once very well-appointed waiting room for long distance passengers. There was not much left of the waiting room's former comfortable fixtures, apart from a couple of armchairs and one

couch. If I were lucky, I would manage to get one of the armchairs, from which I would stare longingly at the hands of the
clock on the wall. I could not wait to get back to Rublevo,
which had become home, to our warm, dry room, to the club
with its constant round of activities—in fact, to the center of
our existence. Even if we had no tea and sugar, we had all the
hot water we needed and could wash as much as we liked. I
thought about my job, about the new friends who had replaced
my lost family, and Moscow held no more attraction for me.

And so time passed until the fateful day which was to
change the entire course of our lives.

It was early spring, but winter was slow in releasing its grip.
Heavy snowfall distorted the roads or covered them completely,
without trace. An evening concert which was to include performers from Moscow had to be canceled. Some said that the
jugglers and acrobats, who were to come with all their gear and
bring a new movie from Moscow, had had to turn back halfway;
others maintained that the performers had accepted an engagement closer to Moscow and used the state of the roads as an
excuse not to travel all the way to Rublevo. Whatever the reason, we found out that there would be no performance only
some three or four hours before the curtain was to rise. To
make matters worse, we had advertised the evening well in advance, and people from surrounding villages were already beginning to drift in with the idea of getting the best seats. A crowd
of young people milled around the club entrance; others strolled
in pairs or in groups around the avenues which had been cleared
of snow. The organizers of all the evenings and educational activities at the club were, of course, our schoolteachers, so it was
up to them to find some way out of the dilemma. Taking me
with them, they went off to the school staff room, to the piano,
having decided that we would stage an impromptu evening
drawing upon our own resources.

A little while later several of the engineers' wives joined us, volunteering their services, and a girl who worked in the accounts office, who had a rather pleasant singing voice. As I have already mentioned, the teacher Alexandra Nikolayevna knew Lyubave's aria from the opera *Sadko* and two of Lel's pieces from *Snowdrop*. Another teacher, who was not a bad violinist, began to rehearse Mendelssohn's darcarole to my accompaniment. The youngest of the teachers—I think her name was Valeria Alexandrovna—had a true, sweet voice and volunteered to sing Rachmaninov's "Lilacs." The wife of one of the engineers, a very handsome, fiery brunette, offered to dress up in a shimmering gown sewn with gold sequins and sing several gypsy songs: "Fly, Horses, Fly!" "Where Tambourines Jingle and Guitars Weep" and even a song from the operetta *Geisha* beginning with the words, "If the little fish plashes and splashes . . ." The gray-whiskered senior teacher offered to read a couple of Chekhov's humorous short stories. Yet even with all these volunteers, we did not have enough acts to fill the time available.

"My mother could sing something!" I exclaimed impulsively, with no thought at all for the possible consequences of my hasty offer.

All the members of the cultural committee stared at me in amazement.

"She sings?" asked somebody.

"Folk songs, I suppose?" asked the engineer's wife with a slightly condescending smile, her tone of voice making it quite clear what she felt about that.

I was showered with questions. A wave of anger welled up in me. I felt deeply offended on my mother's behalf.

"My mother has a classical repertoire, she's a singer," I said, struggling to keep my voice steady.

"Did she study somewhere? What kind of voice does she have? Why didn't we know anything about this before?"

"My mother graduated from the Moscow Philharmonic together with Leonid Vitalyevich Sobinov. She studied under Professor Bezhevich, and for her final examinations she sang the balcony scene from *Romeo and Juliet* with Sobinov!" I blurted out, and then rushed on with reckless abandon. "After that, my mother went on to further her career in Italy and made her debut there at La Scala in Milan. She sang Michaela's part in *Carmen* and the title role in *Tosca*. Then she gave her first solo concerts in Palermo . . ."

An exploding bomb could not have produced a greater impact than my disclosures. But there could be no retraction. The words had been spoken.

My poor, flustered mother could not withstand the entreaties of those who came to seek her out in the Rublevo canteen. Small, frail, but straight as an arrow, she stood there in her white coat beside the steaming pots in the kitchen, trying to wave aside the requests to sing, looking like a white bird flapping its wings. But they would not take no for an answer, and in the end she had to give in.

We repaired to our room, and Mother put on the one black dress which had found its way into our bundle. I crawled around her on my knees, setting pins. This was a dress my mother had worn under a white coat when she had worked as a volunteer nurse in 1914. The style had long since gone out of fashion, and it was a little on the long side. I pinned it up quickly and added a white lace collar. The final effect was pleasingly modest and attractive. What luck that the lace collar had also been thrust into that bundle! As I worked, Mother scolded me without pause, and I dared not lift my eyes to look at her.

"You have no conscience whatsoever!" she repeated. "How did you dare force me into this performance? You haven't even completed your education, but you fancy yourself a teacher! It wouldn't surprise me if you were to take to tightrope walking or stand on your head before all and sundry! Nothing you might do could surprise me, nothing! But what right do you have to make commitments for me?"

She went on and on, recalling all my childhood misdeeds

(like the time I had secretly rigged up a trapeze in the attic and swung on it upside down) and ended up by describing me as the cause of all her troubles. This, however, was more than I could stand.

"You have told me time and again that it's our duty to be useful to everyone, everywhere. Am I asking you to sing at a private party in some engineer's home? The situation is critical. You know that the artists from Moscow have let us down, don't you? You know that means the whole evening is under threat? The club isn't some private enterprise. You're going to be singing for everyone!"

"All right, all right. I know you're a talented advocate!" she responded with a smile and stopped upbraiding me.

Half an hour before the start of the concert we went off to rehearse. I realized that it would not be easy for Mother to sing again after such a long break, after all that she had endured, and in a totally unaccustomed setting. When I sat down at the piano and opened the notes for the standard vocal exercises, I was dismayed to hear how dull her voice sounded, how indifferent she seemed.

Does this mean the end of everything? I thought in dismay, wondering whether she would ever be able to sing again the way she used to. Then she switched to the first arpeggio, then the second, then the third, higher, higher . . . until suddenly her voice cleared and rang out with all its former glory and fullness, catching and carrying her along. There was color in her cheeks, her eyes shone, and she looked years younger. My worries were needless, and I reached calmly for the folder with her repertoire.

The Rublevo audience was disappointed. Instead of the awaited artists from Moscow, the familiar faces of the local teachers appeared, one after another, on the stage. Still, they settled down and began to enjoy themselves. There was much laughter when the usually dour senior master enacted the roles of Chekhov's comic personages.

Just before the first interval Mama came out on the stage.

Her appearance met with a deadly, bewildered silence. Then muffled giggles broke out here and there. This was not surprising. After all, in the minds of the people of Rublevo, Mama was associated with their canteen, with piles of dishes. So what was the meaning of this? How did she have the gall . . . ?

Somewhat uncertainly, I began the introduction to one of Vasili Kalinnikov's romances.

"A sharp axe has wounded the birch tree . . . tears flow down its silvery bark . . ." I heard Mama's voice. When the singer's voice flows with the melody, the accompaniment sounds like the measured blows of tempered steel, then passes into smooth, broad harmony.

"Weep not birch tree, do not grieve! The wound is not mortal, it shall heal by summer . . ." sang Mother, her voice flowing and true in the total silence of the auditorium. The public listened spellbound.

After an explosion of rapturous applause, the hall resounded to the magic melody of Rachmaninov's romance "Spring Waters." "Spring is coming! Spring is coming! We are the young heralds of Spring, sent to prepare her path!" Mama's voice swelled and soared, each not perfect and rising to the roof. She followed with Glière's romance "Live! We shall live!" On the words "We shall move freely into the unknown!" her clear, high voice flooded the hall. I needed to push myself to the limit to keep pace, but luckily Mama's magnificent voice masked the deficiencies of my accompaniment. My eyes were full of happy tears.

My joy was not because of the wild applause or the cries of "Encore"—I was overjoyed for Mama's sake. Until those moments it had seemed to me that something vital inside her had died, as though the sufferings she had endured had burned her out. Yet now she seemed to have discovered new strength, new joy, new inspiration. Tired, worn, battered by fate, she seemed to rise out of the ashes of her former bleak self before my eyes, young, bright, vibrant.

Watching the rapturous reaction of the audience, I tried to analyze the reasons for it. Could it possibly be due just to the unexpectedness of the situation? Was it just the public's surprise that this unobtrusive, reserved, not so young woman who served their meals in the canteen suddenly appeared and sang on stage "like a real artist"? Could surprise alone explain such over-whelming manifestations of appreciation?

After the intermission, I realized that I had been wrong in my skeptical conjectures. These ordinary people, ordinary workers, had a fine feeling for real artistry, an instinctive un-derstanding of it. They sensed that amateur concert or not, they were seeing a real artist perform, and they appreciated both her voice and her dramatic interpretation. Later Mother sang Mar-garita's aria "At spinning, spinning . . ." and Tosca's aria "I de-voted my life to the stage and to love. . . ."

When she went backstage, Mother was positively mobbed. The Rublevo intelligentsia pressed around her, the engineers' wives showered her with kisses, everyone tried to shake her hand, asking why she had not come forward earlier. We were showered with invitations to come round for a cup of tea after the concert was over, but we refused, as we had never socialized with any of them before.

I shall never forget that memorable evening.

At last we managed to get away, back to our own building and our own room. The expression on Mama's face reminded me of how I had seen her in my childhood. She was still flushed and excited. As usual, though, she was displeased with me.

"What on earth possessed you to start all this?" she com-plained. "What for? They could have managed perfectly well without me. What have you done? Now there'll be speculation, questions, suppositions . . . We were getting on so well, living quietly, working, everything was fine, but now . . . !"

"Mama, Mama." I comforted her, kissing her. "Don't worry! Everything will be all right! You'll see! Nothing can go wrong! Nothing!"

I felt light and gay, as though I had just witnessed something miraculous, unexpected, wonderful. I could see a reflection of these feelings in Mama's face, and I feared that at any moment it would go away, leaving behind the tired, drained woman of recent months.

We set about having our dinner. A small saucepan of potatoes we had cooked earlier and then wrapped in newspapers and a blanket sat on one of our mattresses. The potatoes had been frostbitten and were covered with blue and pinkish spots. They were slippery and difficult to peel. A pleasant, slightly sweet smell rose from the saucepan. We ate our potatoes with "tea"—that is, hot water with a small, very dark piece of dried beet instead of sugar. In those days, this seemed an absolute feast, and we were happy that we were providing for ourselves.

On the next day, Mama was summoned by the workers committee of the Rublevo water works.

"How is it that you came to be here?" she was asked when she reported, in some trepidation, in answer to the summons.

"I was directed here by the labor exchange," she replied.

"I know that!" exclaimed the chairman. "As far as I can recall, you came here to take up the job of senior cook, not even canteen supervisor?"

"That's right."

"Why? What on earth made you, a highly educated woman, apply for such a job? It's totally unsuitable for you."

"The labor exchange could not offer me anything else."

"But why?"

Mother remained silent.

"Why?" persisted the chairman. "Please give me an honest answer. I'm not asking you as a superior, but as a comrade. Why?"

"That was all I could qualify for. They wouldn't trust me with anything else."

"But as far as we can see, you are obviously a singer, first and foremost," persisted the chairman with a strange severity. "The canteen is no place for you. You have proved yourself a good, honest worker, an excellent cook, and we would like to improve your lot. There is a great need for competent people to engage in cultural work, and we advise you to go to Moscow. We'll give you a recommendation to the Union of Artists. They'll give you a rating, you'll become a teacher and can teach our young people to sing the way you do . . . We feel it is our duty to help you achieve this. Give it some thought, and let us know your decision!"

Dear, friendly Rublevo! How hard it would be to leave. We had become accustomed to living here; it was ours. We had won a place for ourselves here.

Mother delayed with her reply. I kept quiet, too. The major factor, probably, in our decision to leave Rublevo after all was that after Mother's performance at the concert there was heightened interest in us. Who were we? people asked. Where had we lived before? What had we done? And so forth . . . The Rublevo intelligentsia displayed more curiosity than anyone else, and yet it was these people 'who had earlier not even bothered to exchange the time of day with us.

It was clear that things could not go on like this for much longer, and one day Mother returned from work and said, "We've got to leave. The chairman of the workers committee asked again about sending me with a recommendation to the Artists' Union. I have no idea how I'm going to cope with something like that . . ."

"I daresay it will be a hundred times easier than the work in the canteen," I answered. "But how are we going to part with all the friends we've made here?"

Every day now seemed full of melancholy significance. I can't really say who were my closest friends among the Rublevo youth, I was deeply attached to them all. I promised to write to them regularly and never, never forget them.

As the time of departure drew near, we remembered our little metal case of valuables. The next time Mama saw Ivan Ivanovich in the canteen (we had become friends with his family in the meantime), she asked him to bring it round.

"I buried it in my shed," he told her. "It has an earthen floor, so it was easy. I'll bring it round this evening."

Our departure was imminent. We had only a few days left to work, but Ivan Ivanovich's "this evening" kept being put off. Either he would say that he had been too busy, or he had forgotten or would produce some other excuse.

"Oh, well," sighed Mother. "I suppose it's my own fault for putting so much temptation his way. Who could resist? I can't really blame him. He's got a big family to provide for, too. The blame is mine, and there's no use crying over spilt milk."

And that very evening Ivan Ivanovich came round, carrying our metal case under his arm.

"Here's the pesky thing!" he said, smiling, as he handed the case to Mama. "I swear, it's got a life of its own! It was as if it had disappeared into the ground entirely, I give you my word! I even marked the spot where I buried it, but the dratted thing just seemed to vanish! I've never seen the like, I haven't! I had to dig up the whole floor before I found it again. Then my shovel hit the lid, thank goodness. Gave me quite a turn. Like a miracle, isn't it?"

Yes, it was a miracle, but the miracle was in that man who stood before us, wiping the sweat off his forehead, tired but beaming with pleasure. He looked at us without a shadow in his kind, honest eyes, and Mama and I could not meet his steady regard.

"Just a moment, though!" said Ivan Ivanovich, suddenly serious, and took the case out of Mama's hands. "You showed me the contents before you gave me the case, so I'd like you to look at them now, to make sure that everything's still there."

Mama smiled radiantly.

"Of course, of course! I'll do so gladly. But won't you sit down?" She motioned him to a stool and pulled out the key to the case.

There followed a lengthy, emotional scene during which Mama tried to persuade Ivan Ivanovich to take something as a gift, until he became quite cross with her. He even raised his voice and got up to leave, but Mama managed to placate him somehow at the last moment, and he stopped, reluctantly, to hear her out.

"You must realize," said Mama, "that if I were asking you to render me a service in the accepted sense, I would have offered to give you some kind of remuneration right away. You saw the receipt, which proves that I was not hiding this jewelry from the Soviet government, but have every right to it. My daughter and I came here to live and work, but things have worked out differently. Now Rublevo is sending me back to Moscow. You have all become such dear, good friends, we have spent so many happy hours with your family, and now you will not even let us make you a small gift as a keepsake! Who knows what the future holds? I hope you will not offend me by refusing."

Many, many years have passed. A lifetime. In those years we lost many important papers for many different reasons, and it is by chance that I have managed to retain a few. I have two official documents, attesting to our "baptism by hard work" in Rublevo. The first is addressed to the Ministry of Education in Moscow from the school at the Rublevo waterworks, testifying that in 1918 I had been qualified to teach singing at the school and that the school requested my appointment to that post. This request was taken to Moscow by one of the teachers, because the ministry would never have sanctioned the appointment of an adolescent with unruly braids. At the end of the request, it is stated that my appointment was essential "because School No. 5 of the Presnensky region is located 15 versts from Moscow, and the frequent need for teachers to travel to the city is beginning to have a detrimental effect on the work of the students." The paper is stamped Rublevo, 17 November 1918.

The second document is dated August 1920 and was issued by the Union of Music Teachers to my mother when the state returned the piano requisitioned from us several years earlier. This document affirms that "Piano serial number 107480, Bechstein, from apartment No. 5, Povarskaya Street, is necessary for approved professional activity, and is therefore not subject to requisition."

Those of our class in Russia who had survived by keeping their heads down, snickered suggestively and shrugged their shoulders: "Just imagine! In 1920 the Bolsheviks *returned* Princess Meshchersky's piano!"

The fact is that as soon as Mother, in all sincerity, joined the working life of the country, she was believed, appreciated, and proved herself useful. The self-centered people who sneered at us were incapable of understanding that our strength lay in our sincerity. You cannot work well if you harbor concealed hatred and thoughts of revenge in your heart, for they will twist your soul, consume you, destroy your humanity. When you give yourself wholeheartedly to your work for the benefit of others, there can be no thought of personal grudges or vengeance, and work becomes a pleasure.

My mother and I were not unique. Many, many others remained in our native land, and our common fate was not an easy one.

The Rublevo document about my appointment as a singing teacher bears yet another stamp, placed there fifteen years later. It is the stamp of another government department altogether. Long and narrow the stamp bears two words in large letters— "PASSPORT ISSUED"—followed by the year, 1933. This was the first year Soviet internal passports were issued, and for most people this was a quick and easy process. You reported in alphabetical order, gave the clerk on duty your identity document, and received a Soviet domestic passport in exchange. But for some people it was not like that. Shortly before that, Mama and I had been dismissed from our jobs, taken into police custody, and separated from each other in solitary cells.

It was by chance that the man who signed the protocol of my last interrogation turned out to be one of the three "criminals" sentenced to internal exile to whom, in the spring of 1914, Mother had given sanctuary.

7

Mama and the
Three "Criminals"

From a distance, the enormous, shady park surrounding our Pokrovskoye estate could easily have been mistaken for a forest. At night, the watchdogs would be let off their chains, and the grounds were patrolled by three watchmen armed with rifles and wooden clappers. As children, we liked to fall asleep reassured by the sound of these clappers, approaching or receding as the watchmen made their rounds.

One cool, moonless night we were suddenly awakened by the frenzied barking of the dogs and a fusillade of shots. The watchmen had caught three strangers in the park. Luckily, it was the watchmen's practice to shoot into the air, more to frighten than to maim. But the dogs, who were the ones who had really effected the capture of the intruders, had bitten their legs quite savagely.

The steward reported to Mama that three escaped convicts had been apprehended. A freight train carrying criminals sentenced to hard labor had been passing by that night. These three men had been traveling in the last car and had pried up several rotten floorboards with the idea of escaping. When the train slowed down to cross over a bridge, they chose their moment and dropped through the aperture they had made onto the tracks. As they were in the last car, they ran no risk of being struck by anything, and the guard who sat dozing on his perch at the back of the train noticed nothing.

Stumbling about in the dark, the runaways thought they saw a forest looming in the distance and headed in that direction for cover. When they reached it, they came up against a wall, which they scaled without pausing to think, and were promptly caught.

Our family doctor administered first aid and disinfected the dog bites. Then the escapees were locked inside the bathhouse, and a guard armed with a rifle was posted outside.

This incident, naturally, caused a sensation in the household. Although the bathhouse stood well away from the main house, everyone was afraid to go outside. If they could not avoid doing so, they would run as fast as they could across the courtyard, crossing themselves and looking back fearfully over their shoulders. Lamps were lit in every room and burned all night. Nobody went back to bed and when the day finally dawned everyone was talking about nothing but the miscreants locked in the bathhouse.

"What shall we do with them?" our steward asked Mama. "Shall we call the constable or take them straight to the regional administration?"

"But who are they?" asked Mama, puzzled. "Have you asked them?"

"Asked them? Those crooks? It's clear enough who they are: they're convicted criminals. They should be turned over to the authorities, that's what!"

"Don't you dare!" ordered Mama angrily. "My orders are that not a word should be said about this, not one word! I don't want anyone to find out about them. Forget they exist!"

"But what do you want me to do with them?" demanded the steward, hardly believing his ears. "What am I to do with them?"

"What do you mean, what? First of all, heat up water and let them wash, then give them clean clothes and burn the ones they are wearing now. Then give them a decent meal, and then . . ." Mama paused for a moment, thinking. "Then you can bring them here to me, all three."

"Here?!"

"Yes, here, to my study. It's quite simple. Well, what are you waiting for?"

"Your Highness!" entreated the steward. "You can't mean that! That's going against the law! They should be put in the hands of the authorities, they're not human, they're criminals. Oh, my goodness!"

"So they're criminals," said Mama calmly and even cheerfully. "I've never seen any criminals in my life, and I want to take a look at them."

Mother's orders were obeyed. Several hours later she was surprised to be confronted by three young men, two Russians and one Jew. They stood on the threshold of her study, eyeing her with suspicion and hostility.

"You must forgive me," said Mama, feeling slightly flustered for some reason. "I have no intention of questioning you, for I daresay you've had enough of that! Nor will I ask your names, because you would probably not tell me, and I don't want to know anyway. All I want to know is what crimes each one of you committed? Why were you sentenced to exile?"

At first there was silence. Then one of them spoke up. "We're from the underground."

"The *underground?*" repeated Mother blankly.

Seeing her total lack of understanding, one of the three explained. "Actually, we are students of Moscow University, and we have been sentenced to internal exile for our political activity."

*M*y father, Prince Alexander Vasilievich Meshchersky, sculpted in bronze by Paolo Trubetskoy. Now in the reserves of the Tretyakov Gallery, Moscow. Taken from me and nationalized, like all sculptures and portraits of my father.

*M*y mother, born Ekaterina Porfirievna Podborskaya, was an accomplished equestrienne.

*M*y father's first wife, Elizaveta Sergeevna Stroganova.

*M*y stepsister, Lily, who married Count Fabrizzio Sasso-Ruffo.

*L*ily's husband, Count Fabrizzio Sasso-Ruffo.

*M*other, Vyacheslav, and me, age four.

*W*ith my pet goat and two school friends, age ten.

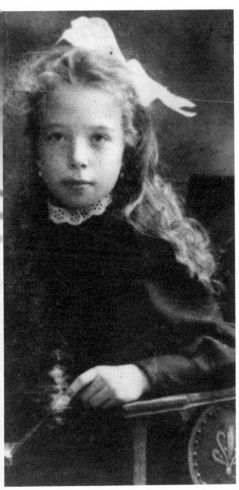

Age ten, in 1914.

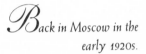

Back in Moscow in the early 1920s.

Teacher of ballroom dancing.

Vesely Podol, the Meshchersky Palace on the estate near Poltava, the Ukraine, showing the heraldic tower.

The picture gallery, Vesely Podol.

"I see! Well, why didn't you say so right away?" cried Mother with relief and launched into conversation with them.

Some five minutes later, the curious household staff peeked through the keyhole to see Mama sitting on the couch with the three "criminals," deep in animated talk.

The students were saying that the people were preparing to overthrow the autocracy, after which all lands would be seized from landowners and class distinctions abolished. Mama heard them out thoughtfully.

"Oh, well," she said finally, "I suppose anything can happen. Fight for your ideas if you think you are right, but what am I supposed to do with you now? Naturally, you're quite safe here. Nobody would dare come searching for you in this place. In any case, it would never enter anyone's head that Princess Meshchersky would hide political offenders, especially those who had escaped after being tried and sentenced. But what now? I am powerless to help you with what you need most—passports. As for anything else, well, you can live here as long as you like. I give you my word that nobody will betray you."

"Thank you for your kindness," they replied. "We'll stay here for a while and then move on. We'll go off one by one."

"Please let me know before you disappear," said Mama. "I'll do whatever I can to help."

The three politicals remained with us until the end of autumn. Nobody informed on them. This was solely because of the respect commanded by Mother. She ordered that they be given rooms in the steward's house and have access to all amenities. The following day they asked Mama for books. She told them to make out a list, and the books were obtained for them without delay. However, this was not enough to suit their needs, and we were forever finding one or another of them perched up on the ladder in our family library. All three immediately instituted a lively correspondence with Moscow and Petrograd. Of course, we all realized that they were not using their real names.

The "criminals" fascinated me, for in my youthful imagination I identified them with Jean Valjean. Despite my governess's disapproval and her acid remarks about bad manners, I would stare at them in wonder whenever we encountered them in the park and would turn my head to follow their progress when they passed. My romantic heart yearned for something sensational. Of course, I did not expect them to steal any silver candlesticks, for that had already been done by Victor Hugo's character, but I could always hope that they might kidnap my nasty governess, and I would be a free agent until a replacement for her was found. Nanny Pashenka's behavior seemed to confirm all my fantasies. Whenever she sighted one of the runaways, even at a distance, she would begin to cross herself feverishly and repeat; "May the Lord protect us! Lord, have mercy, protect and save us!"

Late at night, sitting by my bedside in the dim light of the lamp before the icons, Nanny would shake her white head, murmuring all the while, "Evil stalks the world, hiding from sight. It finds itself a cozy nook and settles there . . ."

Her eyes would be raised to the icons. The light of the lamp was reflected in her large, tear-filled, light blue eyes, and little tendrils of hair shone around her head in the uncertain light like a halo.

"She has sinned, our princess," murmured Nanny. "Sinned before God and the tsar, taken a heavy burden on her angelic soul, a white dove has taken in black ravens. Grief there'll be from it . . . grief . . ."

The following morning, I would stare my eyes out at the "black ravens" again, and feel disappointed. They were perfectly ordinary looking young men, and there was nothing menacing or mysterious about them at all. After a while, I lost interest in them.

In the meantime, the politicals were doing very nicely for themselves. In the evenings, Mama would often sit talking to them on a bench in the park, or if we had no visitors, they would drink tea with us. They chose books for Mother to read.

I remember one such book lying on a table in the drawing room and peeked at the title: it was Nikolai Chernyshevsky's novel *What Is to Be Done?*

The feast of Saints Peter and Paul was the feast day of the church in Petrovskoye. As usual on that day, there was a banquet for the clergy and representatives of the local authorities after the Holy Liturgy. Before tea was served, the head of the district council went for a stroll in the park and came face to face with the "criminals," who were sitting in one of the pavilions reading.

"Princess," he asked politely, "who are these young men? I don't recall seeing them at the table."

"No, they were not there. They're guests of my steward's son—a nephew and two of his friends."

There were no further questions.

In late autumn, just before the return to Moscow, the politicals disappeared. Each one came to bid Mother good-bye. I was not present on any one of these occasions, so I cannot repeat what was said, but I do know that they all received food and clothes for the journey, and 250 rubles in cash each. Mama also wanted them to take a valise with a pillow and blanket, but they declined this offer.

"No, that's impossible! We want to look like holiday makers and not arouse any suspicion."

Autumn that year was very cold and unpleasant; fine days were few and far between. The avenues in the park were covered with fallen leaves which did not rustle underfoot, but lay in a solid, soggy mess. Mama seemed pensive and sad. We began to light stoves for warmth in the long autumn evenings and frequently sat around the fireplace. But there were no more endless, amusing discussions and stories. Something seemed lacking.

The politicals were not to be mentioned from the first day they appeared, and nobody said a word about them now, either. However, we all remembered these people who had come into our lives so unexpectedly, and then disappeared into the unknown without a trace.

The year 1933 was the worst, the darkest year for all the çi-devants, members of the former aristocracy still living in Moscow. It was known that none of them, especially those who were titled, would be issued passports or have the right to live in Moscow. Those against whom there were charges were arrested in advance, and the rest were to be relocated over a hundred kilometers from Moscow—that is, if they were lucky enough not to have anyone inform against them and aggravate their predicament. It is a sad fact that there were people who took advantage of this situation to settle personal grudges and advance their own careers. In most cases, all such reports were pure invention.

Dzerzhinsky, who remembered the business with the Botticelli Madonna and who had helped us out on many occasions, was no longer alive. Therefore, we, too, were overtaken by the fate which befell so many.

First, Mother and I were dismissed from our jobs. Then the administration put our names on the list of those in our building who had been "dispossessed." There were only three of us on that list: the former famous goldsmith M. V. Kishinevsky, who had once had a shop on the Arbat, Mother, and I.

On the day appointed for the issue of passports, the club run by our building administration began to fill with people. It was so crowded that not everyone could get in, and some had to stand outside. The commission issuing passports did not sit in the auditorium, but in the dressing rooms behind the stage. Periodically, the assistant secretary would emerge and call the surname of the next person to come forward. The commission would issue a passport—these, as I have said, were the first Soviet passports—in exchange for old identity papers.

The day passed incredibly slowly. Toward evening, the letters "K" and "M" had long been completed, but nobody had called our names. We sat with Kishinevsky in that empty, stuffy room which reeked of tobacco, and awaited our fate.

Suddenly the door leading into the auditorium flew open. Two uniformed men strode in, ascended the stage, and entered the room where the passport commission was conducting its business.

Moments later, we were summoned. After a few brief questions, the members of the commission took our identity documents, gave us nothing in exchange, and told us curtly to go with the two soldiers. We were taken through the emergency exit into the backyard, where a closed van was already waiting, one of the all-too-familiar "Black Marias."

We could barely stand on our feet, we were so exhausted, and had been too nervous all day to eat anything. When the van moved off, I thought that I would never walk the streets of Moscow again and look upon my beloved city.

We were delivered straight to the Lubyanka, where they locked us into cells in the basement. Mama and I were separated, and this was harder to bear than anything else.

I sat in a solitary cell. Interrogations were conducted at night. Sleep was impossible. I knew quite well why we had been brought straight to the Lubyanka prison, rather than to another of the prisons, such as the Butyrskaya or Taganka, where we had been incarcerated on a number of earlier occasions. The first Soviet passports were to be issued only to those who were considered totally above suspicion. Those who were thought to be in some way questionable or possibly untrustworthy were to be swept aside, or rather thrown out of the Soviet capital. There was only one place for us to go from the Lubyanka—into internal exile, and in those days it did not take long to fabricate a "case" against anyone.

The charges preferred against me were as ludicrous as they were monstrous. It was alleged that I had agitated against the Soviet regime and called for an uprising; I had links with people abroad and was planning to restore some surviving Romanov on the throne; I was a member of some mysterious "group of five" in Moscow—I had allegedly made no secret of that fact, had talked about it in front of witnesses. Some of my supposed fellow conspirators from this "group" had already been arrested, I was told, and had confessed to everything, naming my name.

At first I only smiled as I listened to this nonsensical slander, but after a number of sleepless nights I began to doubt my own sanity. When, after yet another cross-examination by three investigators I refused to sign the list of "crimes" with which I was charged—and which I had never committed—they informed me that under Article 58 of the Criminal Code and various other articles I would be exiled to the Far North for ten years.

"The length of your sentence could be reduced if you confess," said one of the investigators with a sour smile.

I refused. Calmly and deliberately, he raised his pen close to his eyes, checked that it was clean, wiped it on the blotter, and silently but imperatively offered it to me. The smile was gone. Again, I refused to sign.

He rose to his feet noisily and pressed a button to summon the guard. Picking up my file, he motioned the guard to lead me on ahead and followed behind. When we reached the elevator, he dismissed the guard and took me up to a higher floor. The elevator stopped smoothly, and we stepped out. My foot slipped on a highly polished parquet floor. I was blinded by the sunlight pouring in through the large windows that ran the length of the corridor.

We entered a huge, carpeted room filled with numerous indoor plants. A uniformed man was seated behind a large desk, hunched over a stack of papers. I caught a glimpse of the marks of rank on his collar, but averted my face. Fatigue made me feel dull and indifferent to what was to come. I was convinced that this was the end, my fate had been decided. All that remained now was to go through empty, meaningless formalities.

In order to stay on my feet, I kept closing my eyes. The

floor seemed to keep rising to meet the ceiling, and the ceiling to stretch down to the floor. I felt dizzy and nauseous—warning signs of a heart attack. As if through a fog, I saw the man sitting at the desk raise his head, glance at me, and heard him tell the investigator, "You can go. I'll let you know if I need you."

The investigator drew himself stiffly to attention like a frightened raw recruit, put my file down on the table, clicked his heels smartly, turned and left.

"Sit down," I heard the same voice. "So you refuse to confess . . . you're refusing to sign . . . to make a clean breast of things . . . claiming you're not guilty . . ."

He spoke slowly, with pauses, sounding indifferent and even rather tired, but at the same time his eyes ran quickly and keenly over the papers in my file.

Suddenly his eyes stopped, almost as if he could not believe something he had just read, then continued to skip over the page.

"Sit down, will you?" he repeated with an edge of irritation in his voice.

Trying not to collapse, not to let him see the trembling of my hands, I felt my way to the chair and sat down. It was huge, made of good leather, and very soft. For a fleeting second I felt a flash of long-forgotten comfort, but then chilled to the thought that I was probably living my last minutes . . . and where was Mama? Where? What had happened to her?

"Now then," said the man at the desk, "tell me about your family, your parents. What relatives do you have? Where are they?"

I had made up my mind not to answer. My fate was sealed anyway. I would surely die before I reached the Far North. I didn't even have a warm coat, boots, or a headscarf. My feet were shod in open shoes, and my coat was an ancient, threadbare garment made from an old army blanket. The outcome was perfectly obvious. So why these questions? Why couldn't he leave me alone?

"What's this? Are you refusing to answer?"

"I have already supplied the answers in written form and repeated them time after time orally."

He looked at me through half-closed eyes, then went on menacingly; "Well, now *I'm* asking you. Are your parents alive?"

"Only my mother."

"And your father?"

"He died before I was born."

"What is your mother's name and patronymic?"

I answered. For some reason, he made a nervous movement and grasped the arms of his chair.

"Did you own estates?"

"I didn't own them, I was only a child . . . why are you asking all this?"

"Never mind, why! I'm asking you, did you own an estate? Where was it? What was it called?"

"There was one near Poltava . . ."

"But was there one not far from Moscow? What was it called?" he interrupted.

I looked up at him and saw that he was clearly in a state of some agitation.

"Well, there were two, along the Bryansk road: Petrovskoye and Pokrovskoye."

"Pokrovskoye . . . Pokrovskoye," he repeated, as though trying to recall something. "Was there a river nearby? With a railway bridge over it?"

Puzzled by his intensity and making an effort to pull myself together, I began to reply, feeling the stirrings of some vague, inexplicable hope. As I talked, his face seemed to lose the stern expression which is the hallmark of all those who have been given the power to question others, and his eyes became quite human. It even seemed as though there was a smile lurking in their depths. He cut me off with a wave of his hand.

"Do you remember a time when your mother gave sanctuary to three runaway political prisoners?"

"Yes."

"Do you, now? Then tell me about it. Go on, tell me in as much detail as you can remember."

That which followed is like some fairytale.

"So you are that little girl who was always being punished for some mischief or other?" he queried quite warmly now, his face lit by a smile. "But where is your mother?"

"She's not in Moscow anymore. They told me during interrogation that she has already been sent away to the Far North, to the Solovki Islands."

"Nonsense, they were only saying that to frighten you!" He smiled again. "It happens, sometimes. She's here, in another cell. Would you like some tea with lemon?" he asked unexpectedly, smiling as if to himself. He came over to me and put a hand on my shoulder. "You see, we meet again!"

He thrust his hands into his pockets and took several turns around the room, watching me out of the corner of his eye. I sat there in shock, not believing my eyes or my ears. He paced back and forth across his large office, head down, almost like an automaton. I could see the expression on his face, but he was clearly in the grip of his own memories, recalling the turbulent, dangerous years of his youth.

We were both remembering the same times.

I came to myself with a start and for a moment couldn't understand where I was. Then it all came flooding back: I was in an office in the Lubyanka, and a stranger in uniform was continuing some conversation of which I couldn't make head or tail as I desperately tried to recall its beginning.

"So . . . so . . ." he repeated slowly, as though making a decision about something. Then he reached across and pushed a black button on his desk. "First of all, you're going to have a cup of tea with lemon and some sandwiches, and in the meantime I'll go through your papers and see if I can find anything to use as a basis for issuing you a passport. And we'll find your mama, we'll definitely do that. By the way, do you have enough money for your tramfare home?"

He found a suitable paper almost immediately. It had been confiscated at the time of the arrest and was among the first in my file.

"There we are!" he exclaimed, showing it to me. "Guard that with your life! Remember, this paper not only exonerates you, it also confirms your right to live in our proletarian state." With these words, he laid the paper on the desk, opened a drawer, took out a long and narrow stamp, inked it, and pressed it firmly to the document.

"Just wait a little bit longer," he said, smiling at me, "and you'll be given a passport on the strength of this paper."

The life-saving document proved to be the request sent by the school in Rublevo to the Ministry of Education on November 17, 1918, asking for approval of my appointment as singing teacher in view of the fact that the school council felt I had passed my probation period successfully.

I have treasured this bit of paper all my life and never parted with it. During the war, when we were being bombed, I carried it against my breast.

However, that was still to come. But then, in 1919, we returned from Rublevo to Moscow, needing to win a place for ourselves there again. Other people were living in our old apartment, number 5, at 22 Povarskaya Street. The only empty room was the cold, unheated kitchen. This kitchen became our new home. The enormous, black iron stove became our double bed.

That is how my mother and I passed through our "baptism by hard work." In the life of Rublevo, we were only a small, fleeting episode, but for us Rublevo opened a new page in the story of our future working life.

Part II

Father and Mother

My Father's Daughter Lily and the Italian Connection

*M*y father, Alexander Vasilyevich Meshchersky, was first married to Elizaveta Sergeevna Stroganova.

The Stroganovs . . . I daresay that this ancient Russian name is known to everyone. They were tall, enterprising workers, well accustomed to toil, who were attracted by the vast expanses of Siberia and dreamed of opening up the rich natural resources beneath its soil. Therefore, they left their peasant holdings and headed for Siberia to seek and exploit its mineral wealth. Their labor and their hands built our first Siberian factories and foundries, which started the production of Russian copper. The rise of the Stroganovs up the heraldic ladder was astounding. Stepping over the three categories of merchant guilds, they divided into two branches: one of these purchased a baronial title abroad; the other was elevated to the rank of count by decree of the Russian tsar.

What an incredible country Russia was! If any title could be purchased abroad, then it could be lost just as easily. If an aristocrat were to become insolvent to the point of selling off his lands and family seat, he would automatically lose his title and retain only his family surname. It was possible to purchase the family crest and name along with the lands of an impoverished aristocrat, and to add that name to one's own. This frequently resulted in highly complicated agglomerations of names, which were as difficult to memorize as they were cumbersome to say. Near the Sukharev Tower, at flea markets, and in other busy public places, it was not uncommon to see a derelict, drunk vagrant who was nonetheless a count or prince, and who, having no roof over his head, would sleep in charity hostels and end up buried in a mass paupers' grave, but still retain his title!

There was also a law in Russia according to which any person, irrespective of his social origins, would be elevated to the ranks of the gentry by being awarded so-called "personal nobility" (*lichnoye dvoryanstvo*) upon completion of a course of study at an institution of higher education, usually a university. But this status would not extend to his wife and offspring. Such was the case with the father of Vladimir Ilyich Lenin. To reward outstanding contributions to society or feats of military valor, however, a family would be endowed with hereditary nobility. As for the Stroganovs, they were later to become connected through marriage to the ruling Romanov dynasty. Yet by the end of the nineteenth century, when our aristocracy became increasingly impoverished, wealthy merchants found it easy to purchase titles and coronets by marrying off their well-dowered daughters to impecunious "social lions." In fairness, it must be added that by that time our merchants bore little resemblance to the characters immortalized in Alexander Ostrovsky's plays, but were well-educated young people who had traveled abroad and absorbed a good deal of Western culture.

My father's first wife, Elizaveta Stroganova ("Liza"), was a quiet, gentle girl who became an exemplary and loving wife. She was a gifted pianist and, although taught at home, received an excellent education. Unfortunately she subscribed to the current fad of the time—Roman Catholicism—and in many of her portraits she is shown holding a small French Bible in her hands. She conducted all her correspondence and kept her diaries in French and admitted frankly that she often thought in that language. Physically she was quite frail and bore my father only one child, a daughter called Natalia, and known in the family as "Lily." Her excessive love for this daughter drove her into an early grave.

There was a strong resemblance between my half sister Lily and myself, although due to the difference in our ages and force of circumstances, we never met or got to know each other. By all accounts she was a pleasant-enough girl, but very quick-tempered, impulsive, and prone to fantasies. In accordance with the custom in many aristocratic families, she was betrothed while still a child to Prince Trubetskoy, and from early adolescence was madly in love with her fiancé. Their wedding, which was to take place amid due pomp and ceremony, was unexpectedly delayed when the tsar summoned Trubetskoy and informed him that he was to go abroad with a group of young diplomats. The tsar told the young prince of this personally and was quite convinced the news would be very welcome, as it opened up the possibility of Trubetskoy's being posted later to one of our embassies abroad. Trubetskoy was understandably disappointed by the postponement of his wedding, but Lily was absolutely distraught. Her fiery, romantic heart craved danger, adventure, and upheavals. That night, when her English governess had gone to bed, Lily cut her hand with a razor blade and, dipping a quill pen into her own blood, wrote her fiancé a frantic letter. She wrote that she could not tolerate the postponement of the wedding and the prospect of waiting in solitude. She said that she was prepared to crop her hair, run away from home, and accompany her fiancé masquerading as his servant. If he did not agree, she threatened to commit suicide.

Perhaps Trubetskoy's love for Lily was cooler than hers for him; perhaps he was frightened by this letter written in blood; perhaps he was disconcerted by such a passionate outburst or, on the contrary, perhaps he loved her too much to risk losing her: but whatever the reason, he immediately rushed over to see her father, bringing the letter with him. He assured his prospective father-in-law that he loved Lily, but feared that with her temperament she could quite easily fall in love with someone else while he was abroad. He asked Father to watch over Lily carefully in his absence and guard her from any undesirable acquaintances, meetings, and influences.

Father was livid with fury, but restrained himself from showing his daughter's fiancé just how ashamed he was of her disgraceful and intemperate conduct. He bade Trubetskoy not to worry, confirmed that the marriage would go ahead as agreed, and promised to keep a close watch on Lily.

No sooner was Trubetskoy out of the house than Lily was summoned to her father's study. He was beside himself with anger and, making no allowances for Lily's nature and feelings, proceeded to vent his fury on her, claiming that she had disgraced him and much more in the same vein. Lily heard him out in silence, maintained a calm demeanor and, unlike most young girls of her time, did not shed so much as one tear of shame or repentance. She stared fixedly at the table, on which her letter to Trubetskoy lay in full view: a letter written in an outburst of passionate despair, a letter which laid bare her heart and which her fiancé had, treacherously, given into the hands of her father.

The day of Trubetskoy's departure was imminent. A farewell reception hosted by the Meshcherskys, as the bride's family, was attended by all the Petersburg nobility. Lily entered, pale but outwardly composed. Trubetskoy hurried impetuously toward her, but she swung her hand wide and dealt him a ringing slap in the face. She then cried out that her fiancé was beneath contempt, that he had betrayed her, that he had handed over her letter to her father, and that she would never marry an aristocrat.

The scandal this caused defies description. As was to be

expected, the engagement was severed. After that, Lily began to lose weight drastically and, as they used to say, "went into a decline." She became weak; she showed no interest in life; she refused food; and the doctors who had been called in to attend her shrugged their shoulders and began to talk about mental illness. It was at this point that her parents decided that Lily might profit from a trip abroad. But the gay social whirl of Paris and Vienna only exhausted her and laid her low with excruciating headaches. Italy, however, proved a different matter. In Italy, Lily seemed a bit more like her usual self; she grew stronger physically and began to smile again. A stay in Venice was to decide her future. Fate took a hand from the very day of their arrival in the city of canals. Princess Meshcherskaya and her daughter, accompanied by Lily's English governess, Miss West, and a maid named Dasha occupied a suite in the most expensive and fashionable hotel on the Grand Canal. Day and night, numerous gondolas of all kinds were tied up along the canal to the elaborate bronze posts which protruded from the dark waters.

The owners of these gondolas—"Venetian coachmen," as gondoliers were called—congregated in a gay, noisy throng around the entrance to the hotel, offering their services to the hotel guests amid much gesticulation and good-natured jostling. On that first morning in Venice, when the princess, Lily, and Miss West walked out onto the steps leading down to the canal, a tall, well-built gondolier appeared before them, seemingly out of nowhere. Without waiting to hear their reply, he ushered the three women through a crowd of his fellows and settled them into his gondola. He looked quite different from the rest of the gondoliers: his clothes were made of expensive black velvet, and the broad silk sash around his waist was edged with a gold fringe. The same black velvet lined his gondola, and its curtains sparkled with intricate gold-thread embroidery. The oars were decorated with carving comparable to the work of a master jeweler.

Giovanni—as the gondolier introduced himself—turned up at the hotel every morning, placing his gondola at the disposal of the three foreign ladies. His shout of *"Evoe!"*—the required warning cry of the gondoliers at canal intersections—sounded more mellow and gentle than the voices of other gondoliers.

"Do you sing?" the princess once asked in Italian. In reply, Giovanni only smiled, showing a flash of strong, white teeth, and began to sing. Soon afterward Miss West noticed that every morning before breakfast, Lily would make her way unobtrusively to the windows facing the Grand Canal in a state of suppressed excitement and would peek out through the curtains at Giovanni's gondola, which would already be down below, waiting. In the meantime, Giovanni proved to be a superb guide, and our travelers could only marvel at the extent of his knowledge. Mooring the gondola at some point of interest, he would talk about his city with a deep and inspired love.

"Oh, Venice," he would cry, "your very name is magic! You are full of surprises, full of enchantment, you are a fairy tale made real! Venice spreads over 118 islands. Two of her five channels to the sea—Porto Lido and Porto Malamocco—are wide enough for oceangoing ships. There are 378 bridges in Venice, the largest of which is the Rialto, dividing the city in half. On its left bank, palazzos stand side by side, decorated with fine reliefs, marble columns, and bright mosaics, with Venetian lanterns hanging under their arches. Wherever the eye can see, the glint of gold reflects in the dancing waters of the canals and casts an aura of magic and mystery over the life of the city. It is hard to imagine that Venice fought cruel and bloody wars, beating back Norsemen, Slavs, and Saracens. She not only defeated her enemies, but sallied forth herself to bring a large part of the northern coast of Italy under her domination, earning the formidable title 'Queen of the Seas.' "

Lily listened to all this with bated breath, while Giovanni continued. "Venice is a living reminder of bright gold coins streaming from richly beaded purses, of precious stones passing from hand to hand, and of that most mysterious and secret treasure of the deep—cold and breathtakingly beautiful pearls, shining like moonlight. Ah, the Venetian woman! Titian's immortal brush captured her hair, its deep glints giving birth to the name 'Venetian gold.' Her skin is white and translucent, and her eyes are usually the blue-green of the waters of the Adriatic on a calm day. . . ."

The princess and her daughter were spellbound by the eloquence of the young gondolier, until the very correct Miss West, who felt that her companions had fallen into some kind of "indecent trance" and suspected the gondolier of undesirable intentions, cleared her throat loudly, and interrupted the young man's outpourings.

"Princess," she suggested, "don't you feel that we should take a rest from looking at the beauties of Venice and listening to stories about it? Perhaps our kind young guide would be good enough to take us to the nearest restaurant?"

"Of course, of course!" agreed the princess hurriedly, rousing herself with more than a little embarrassment.

It was, in fact, time for lunch, but what was to be done about Giovanni? He had been so attentive, so courteous, how could they possibly expect him to wait outside, tired and hungry as he must be, while they ate? Yet how was it possible to invite this unknown gondolier to share their table? That was simply unacceptable!

Then the princess thought she had found a way out of the predicament. Reaching into her handbag, she drew out a large banknote, one that would have easily paid for a number of dinners, and offered it to Giovanni.

"Please take this," she said to him. "You are a young man, and you need a good, nourishing meal and some wine to go with it. As for us, we're vegetarians and, furthermore, never have wine on the table. I hope you don't mind . . . and that you will drink our health!"

He hung his head, but this did not hide the flush of indignation that darkened his olive skin.

In the restaurant, Lily flatly refused to eat.

"I am not at all hungry anymore," she told her mother. "I have been so happy here. We're not in Russia, where noble rank defines one's place at the table. And even if it were so here, too, then you, a Russian princess, should have shown generosity and goodwill as a sign of thanks to that young Italian. Oh, how right Tsar Peter the Great was! He paid no attention to Russian prejudices and brought ordinary, talented people to his country and then endowed them with noble rank—"

"Your mother, thank God, is not Peter the Great," interrupted Miss West maliciously. "And that sly Italian's talent lies in the fact that he has learned the guidebooks by heart and then beguiles naive foreigners with his knowledge!"

They returned to the hotel in silence. That evening, when Lily retired to her room, Miss West slipped out into the corridor and knocked on the door of the room occupied by the princess. She was still awake and greeted Miss West with words of complaint. "Do you know, that insolent Italian returned the money I had given him to buy himself lunch? He pushed the banknote into my hand when he was helping me climb out of the gondola on our return to the hotel!"

Miss West needed no further encouragement. Casting aside her usual English sangfroid, she confided with alarm that she had been keeping a close watch on the two young people but had said nothing to the princess until now, not wishing to upset her. However, she had no doubt about the passionate looks they exchanged, and she feared that Lily might be in danger of disgracing herself: either the gondolier would spirit her away, or she would go to him herself. Lily's intemperate nature was no secret. It was enough to recall the uproar she had caused by her treatment of her fiancé Prince Trubetskoy in Petersburg! It was essential, insisted Miss West, to take immediate and drastic steps to avert a catastrophe.

The princess listened to Miss West in silence and then reached for the bellpull.

"Bring me all the bills for our stay," she ordered the lackey who appeared in answer to her summons. "I know it's late, but I should also like to have a courier sent round to reserve a separate compartment for the first train leaving for Palermo tomorrow. We are leaving."

Then she woke up her maid Dasha and ordered her to pack all their things as quickly as possible.

When the travelers alighted from the train in Palermo and handed over their luggage to a porter, they had not gone more than a few steps when an elegant young man in a white suit jumped out of the front carriage and barred their path. Raising his hat, he bowed deeply to the princess.

"I am not Giovanni," he told her. "My real name is Fabrizzio, and I am the only son of Duke Sasso-Ruffo. I would like to ask for your daughter's hand in marriage."

Lily would have been glad to cast herself into his arms without waiting for her mother's reaction, but she was a little hurt. She regretted that he was not a simple gondolier after all, especially as she had vowed never to marry an aristocrat. She was also somewhat put out that he had not told her his real name until now.

The princess and Miss West had forgotten that Dasha was with them in Venice. The maid was devoted to Lily and carried notes to Lily every night from the enamored young gondolier. It was she who informed him of the secret flight intended by the princess. Yes . . . Fabrizzio really was the only son of a famous Venetian magnate. Just as the sons of Russian gentry were mad about equestrian sports and idolized their favorite horses, so did Fabrizzio feel about his gondola. He loved nothing better than to spend hours cruising along the waterways of his native city, poling along its canals as far as the warm waves of the Adriatic, which had nurtured and raised him like a solicitous nurse, and made him an outstanding swimmer and boatman. He worshipped the sea and his native Venice, was well known to all the city's gondoliers, and considered them his friends.

He had caught a chance glimpse of the Russian princess and her companions on their arrival in Venice and determined then and there not to let them out of his sight. To achieve this, he decided to become their "Venetian coachman." He gained much secret amusement from listening to the discussions between the princess and her companions. They conversed in English and in French, and it did not enter their heads that a simple Italian gondolier might understand what they were saying. This gave Fabrizzio the opportunity to form an accurate assessment of the character, likes, and dislikes of each one of his passengers. Lily's unusual and resolute character captured his heart.

It is not surprising that the metamorphosis of the gondolier into the son of an Italian duke asking for her daughter's hand in marriage stunned the princess so much that she took what she felt to be the only course of action: she cut short the trip and went straight back to Russia. She told Fabrizzio that she could not give her consent; that decision rested with her husband. Therefore, it was up to Fabrizzio to come to Russia and repeat his proposal to Lily's father.

As it happened, the prince, who had been warned what to expect in a lengthy telegram sent by the princess, was in a towering rage.

"My daughter marry an Italian? Never!" was his reaction. "Surely a suitable husband can be found for her here, in Russia, one who would be Russian both in spirit and in faith?"

However, when the young Italian nobleman arrived posthaste, he managed to charm his prospective father-in-law into acquiescence.

As the Dowager Empress Maria Fyodorovna expressed a desire to give the young couple her blessings personally, the Meshcherskys had to travel to Petersburg, and the wedding was to take place in Saint Isaac's cathedral. They stayed with Father's older brother, Boris, on Millionnaya Street.

"It was a glittering, unforgettable wedding," recounted ninety-year old Aunt Olga Vasilyevna Solovyeva, former atten-

dant to the princess, who had a small grace-and-favor house by
the river on the Meshcherskys' Petrovskoye estate. "The number of people who attended . . . ! It took our Russian maids and
their Italian counterparts one and a half hours to dress the bride.
The dowager empress blessed the bride and groom with an icon
decorated with Russian freshwater seed pearls, and two palace
footmen presented the bride with a mother-of-pearl casket lined
with black velvet on which lay a sparkling diamond parure. And
the groom! He was so unbelievably handsome, one look from
his eyes was enough to turn your bones to water!"

Immediately after the wedding, the young couple boarded
the night train to Italy, where Lily entered upon a life of pomp
and splendor in the family palazzo of the Sasso-Ruffos.

However, she paid visits to Russia from time to time. Lily
proved to be a loving wife and tender mother and bore the duke
three daughters: Helena ("Elsa"), Maria, and Olga. But more
about them later. Prince Meshchersky was delighted by the way
things had turned out.

Whenever Lily came to visit her former homeland, she
always brought a large retinue of Italian servants, one of whom
was a famed pastry cook–confectioner called Giacomino. He
developed a taste for Russian vodka and took to drinking with
the servants in his free time. Alas, he did not realize that in this
he was no equal to his Russian cup-companions. They could
down drink for drink with him and remain in control of themselves, whereas poor Giacomino would down his third glass and
then leap up, eyes starting from his head, and either try to
provoke a fight or seize a meat cleaver and chase after the first
person to catch his eye. This would go on until our coachmen
would overpower him, tie him up, and then drag him off to the
stables to "sleep it off."

But Lily's married happiness did not endure, and a rift occurred between her and the husband she had adored. It started
when she became certain that the duke had a mistress, with
whom he had no intention of parting, among the Italian servants

who surrounded her day and night. Later more of Fabrizzio's infidelities came to light. Divorce was unthinkable in those days, and Lily, with her proud and impetuous nature, was not one of those wives who are prepared to close their eyes to their husband's peccadilloes. They began to lead separate lives under the same roof, "in two separate wings," as they used to call it then. The duchess would descend to the carriage waiting outside her wing, just as the duke would arrive from some unknown place on horseback to dismount outside his wing. Of course, outward appearances were maintained. They would attend social functions together, her hand on his arm. They would talk as if nothing was wrong, even though everybody knew the true state of affairs between them.

It is not hard to imagine how Lily, with her forthright nature and her love for the duke, suffered. Possibly in the hope of making the duke jealous, or to gain a measure of revenge, or to show the world that she didn't care, Lily began to pay the duke back in his own coin. But if society was prepared to overlook the philanderings of unfaithful husbands, unfaithful wives were condemned without mercy. It is hard to say what Lily's defiant behavior would have brought about (it was whispered that she would be forbidden to appear at the royal court) if something had not occurred to break up the ducal family once and for all.

Prince Meshchersky had a close friend in a very well-known family of Poltava landowners, May-Boroda, who had fallen on hard times. This friend begged Prince Meshchersky to do something to save his only grandson, who faced imminent ruin. This grandson, an incredibly handsome young man, was an officer in one of the most elite Guards regiments. Like far too many of his kind, he became addicted to drinking and cards and lost a huge sum gambling with regimental funds. The embezzlement was hushed up and the missing money somehow returned, but there was no question of the culprit's remaining in the regiment.

Having resigned his commission, he was now at loose ends, and it was imperative to find him some kind of employment.

"Let it be something involving hard work," his grandfather urged the prince. "Just ordinary work, for which he will get his monthly wages and learn what it means to earn his own living. I beg you," continued the distraught old man, "fix him up with something! You have three estates, surely you could give him some job in one of the estate offices? If he is taken away from the city, sent to the countryside, where there is plenty of fresh air and natural beauty, he might change for the better."

"But I have no such position," answered the prince uneasily. "Especially for a former officer of the Guards . . ."

"Maybe he could be a night watchman? I'll make him atone for his wrongdoing! It took every penny I possess to return the money he gambled away to the regiment and to save our whole family from being blackened by his folly. I beg you, my friend, help me in this!"

Unable to resist the pleas of his friend, the prince took the young man on as a steward of his Pokrovskoye estate and paid him a generous salary. Little did he know what tragic consequences his good deed was to have! It was not long before it became common knowledge that the young man had become Lily's lover. The prince was crushed by the shame of having his married daughter's lover living there under the same roof, in front of his three growing granddaughters, while the servants, who always know about such matters down to the smallest details, snickered. The owners of the neighboring estates, too, were all fully aware of what was going on.

As could have been expected, the prince immediately dismissed the young man from the steward's post, but as soon as he had done so, Lily announced that she was going abroad for an indefinite period. This was right in the middle of winter, in the crackling cold just before New Years. The princess, never robust, had just recovered from a long and severe bout of influenza. In order to try to salvage at least some remnants of Lily's reputation, she decided to accompany her daughter, if only for the sake of preserving an outward appearance of propriety. She also managed to persuade Lily's young lover to travel ahead alone and wait for Lily in Paris. The princess went with Lily as far as the border and then returned home. However, she was forced to take to her bed immediately, for she had caught another heavy cold during the journey. This cold developed rapidly into pneumonia, and the combination of a raging fever and the mental anguish that had weakened her heart proved to be her death. Lily did not return to Russia for her mother's funeral, and several months later sent for her three daughters with their nannies and governesses to join her abroad.

Having buried his wife and finding himself abandoned by his daughter and beloved granddaughters, the prince resolved not to remarry. He began to devote himself fully to social activities, especially as at this time he was elected marshal of the Moscow nobility. Like all the Meshcherskys, however, he was an ardent lover of the arts, and affairs of state alone were insufficient to absorb all his interest. His wealth made it possible for him to become one of the leading patrons of the arts in Moscow, seeking out and encouraging the development of the many new talents burgeoning in Russia at that time. This gave meaning and added color to his life.

Such was my father, and such was his lifestyle when he met his future wife, my mother.

9
The Wodzinskys
and the Podborskys

*M*y maternal grandmother was from a noble but long-impoverished Polish family, the Wodzinskys. Their salons had been famous for concerts featuring performances of some of the most outstanding singers and pianists of their time. For instance, Chopin frequently played at the Wodzinskys' and later taught piano to one of the enchanting young daughters of the house. He was more than a little in love with her and dedicated one of his compositions to her.

As a member of the Wodzinsky family, Grandmother inherited a family heirloom, a small bronze bust of Chopin and a cast of his hand. Like all girls of her class, Grandmother studied in a select girls school attached to a convent, and she received a brilliant education. Apart from foreign languages and all the usual subjects, the girls were taught to paint on silk and porcelain, to do exquisite embroidery, and also to master the fascinating art of making flowers not just from paper and fabric, but also from wax. Alas, these many talents were not to be put to use in the difficult life that marriage was to bring. Her marriage to my grandfather was a classical love match. For his sake, she abandoned the Roman Catholic faith and embraced Russian Orthodoxy; Jadvyga Wodzinksa became Nadezhda Podborskaya, the wife of a humble district doctor on a small salary. They lived on the brink of poverty, in an apartment which came with the job, surrounded by eight children, unable to afford more than one servant. Making ends meet toward the end of every month, while maintaining a "respectable" front, was a recurrent nightmare.

Nadezhda was a quick-tempered, proud, and rather ambitious woman who could not accept her husband's seeming satisfaction with this lifestyle. She constantly reproached him for his lack of ambition and for not seeking the aid of his many influential patients in securing a transfer to the capital. She would often enact hysterical scenes when he would ignore the summons of a wealthy patient and go off in a peasant's cart to some far-off village where he had been called to help.

I never knew my grandfather, but I revere his memory deeply. He was a retired general, a military man, but his first love was medicine (he was a graduate of the Medical Academy), and it was to this that he devoted his entire life.

The Polish Podborsky family had risen in rebellion against Russia on numerous occasions, shedding much blood but retaining a stubborn unwillingness to accept Russian domination. At the same time, Poland was constantly under attack by the Ukrainian *hetmen*. The Podborskys were descended from the Lithuanian king, Gediminas, but incessant internecine strife had exhausted the family's wealth and ended with the loss of their lands; by foreign custom this also lost them their count's crest. As it happened, my grandfather was the first such "non-count" Podborsky.

When Mama married Prince Meshchersky, he immediately offered to have Grandfather reinstated to his rightful rank and to buy back Podboryane, the famous Podborsky estates near Bender, thereby securing the return of the family crest. Grandfather thanked his son-in-law for his generosity, but made his own position quite clear.

"Believe me, Prince," he said, "I have no interest whatsoever in the title. My mission in life is to help people, to ease their sufferings, and being a good doctor is of far greater importance to me than worldly honors."

Grandfather was a devout Christian and a human being in the best sense of the word: he was kind, gentle, honorable, a loving husband and devoted father. It was not unknown for him to leave his own money by the bedside of a poor patient. The only object he had that was of any material worth—a gold watch with a diamond imperial eagle on the case, awarded to him by the tsar for military valor—was invariably with the pawnbrokers. He got by with an ordinary steel watch purchased during his student days at university. He did much good, but always sought to hide it. Our grandmother only realized the extent of his charity when she saw the huge crowd of people who came to pay their last respects to him at his funeral. He had helped each and every one of them at some time. When the moment came to remove the coffin from the church, the people hoisted it up on their shoulders and carried it to the cemetery. As a doctor, Grandfather knew he was dying of cancer of the liver, a lingering and painful death. However, he kept it a secret from his wife and children, suffering in silence for as long as he could. He assured Grandmother that all he had was gall bladder trouble, which is painful but nonetheless curable. Shortly before Grandfather finally had to take to his bed, the family suffered a severe blow—the death of the youngest son, six-year-old Anatoli. He was a universal favorite, this quiet, gentle, fair-haired little boy. He was everyone's pet, not only because he was the youngest but because even strangers would say, looking at his wistful little face and shy smile, "He's not long for this world . . . his like never live long." Nothing Grandfather or his colleagues could do saved him from dying from scarlet fever with complications to the heart.

As he lay in his little bed, he kept asking his mother to teach him the words of the Lord's Prayer, which he found hard to memorize.

"Don't strain yourself," Grandmother would say, kissing him. "You're sick now, and you've got a temperature. When you get well again, you will learn the prayer very easily."

"But I have to learn it now," he insisted tearfully. "How can I go to Jesus if I don't know His prayer?! Please, Mama, say it, and I'll repeat it after you."

He died whispering the words "Thy will be done . . ." When Grandfather finally collapsed soon after Anatoli's death, the spiritual bond between those two remained unbroken.

In order to prepare Grandmother for her husband's death, the doctors decided to tell her the truth, especially since the injections of morphine, which had been used to subdue the worst of his pain, were now insufficient. Yet about two weeks before Grandfather's death, the pains suddenly seemed to lessen.

"Prokofi Semyonovich," said Grandfather's colleagues to him, "what is it you're taking? Surely you can tell us, your fellow doctors?"

He would only shrug and smile, but once he confided to Grandmother, "When the pains become unbearable, Tolya comes and stands at the head of my bed and rests his cool little fingers on my burning forehead and kisses me. And then all the pain recedes, and I go to sleep."

One morning, Grandfather ordered candles to be bought for the church and asked the priest to hear his confession and administer the Blessed Sacrament.

"Tonight is my last night on this earth," he said. "Light lamps and candles by all the icons, gather around my bed, and take turns reading the Gospels aloud."

They did as he asked, and toward morning he seemed to drift into unconsciousness. Grandmother sat by his side, holding his hand. Suddenly his eyes flew wide open, and his fingers tightened painfully around hers. He looked straight into the corner where the icons stood and cried out in a firm, glad voice, "I believe, Lord! I see!"

"Who do you see? Who?" asked Grandmother, trembling.

"Shhhh . . ." he whispered, putting a finger to his lips. A smile of pure happiness lit up his face like a ray of sunshine. He closed his eyes and lay back quietly on his pillows. That is how Grandfather died.

Now that I have acquainted the reader with the main characters who will figure in these memoirs, it remains for me to fill in some details about the composition of the Podborsky family at the time when Prince Alexander Meshchersky came into their lives. Two more Podborsky children had died by that time during a dysentery epidemic, leaving only five: three daughters and two sons. The eldest daughter, Olga, was very plain but extremely intelligent. She was awarded a gold medal upon completion of secondary school and went on to graduate from two faculties at university: foreign languages (German and French) and the historico-philological faculty. She wrote quite good poetry, which was published here and there in journals and was Grandmother's pride and joy. The youngest, Anatolia (so called in memory of little Anatoli, who had died), was exceptionally beautiful. She was taught music, singing, drawing, sculpture, and especially dancing. In other words, all the resources available were spent on the oldest and the youngest daughters.

The middle daughter, Catherine (who was to be my mother), seemed to be endowed with no particular talents. Her thin, mobile face gave no hint of her future beauty. Her luxuriant chestnut hair, which shone with gold highlights, only provoked her brothers into dubbing her "Ginger Cat." Her biggest fault was thought to be an unfailing determination always to speak her mind, not necessarily an endearing characteristic. Grandmother considered Catherine's predilection for plain speaking a sign of bad manners and punished her for it. However, punishment brought about no change, and Grandmother finally decided that her second daughter was incorrigible. But Catherine, "Katya," was Grandfather's favorite among his children, a fact he never tried to hide. From him she inherited her amazing kindness, lack of vanity, sincerity—characteristics which meant, in Grandmother's estimation, that her intelligence was limited and she was a poor little dab of a creature.

Olga's intellectual attainments and Anatolia's beauty gave Grandmother hopes of finally rising above poverty. She dreamed of arranging brilliant marriages for them, which would enable her to return to the social circles into which she had been born and in which she had spent her childhood. Surely it was this for which she prayed before the icon of the Black Madonna of Czestochowa, her family icon, the Polish *Matka Boska,* Mother of God.

In the meantime, Katya was the Cinderella of the family in the full sense of the word. She would sit up nights helping Grandmother sew ball dresses for Olga. If she were to fall asleep over this task, she would be woken by a sharp reprimand from her mother. Katya helped do the family wash and cleaned the floors if the servant was out sick. It was she who had to run to the shops, singing from morning till night. Like a bird, she found it impossible not to sing. But there was not enough money for Katya's education, so she was sent to the diocesan school, which took her in immediately because of her high, pure voice. Unlike her sisters, she had no girlfriends but preferred the company of her brothers, taking part in their games and mock battles. To Grandmother this tomboy behavior betokened a hoyden, and more than once she expressed the wish that it were possible to consign Katya to a nunnery.

"That's the only place for her," she would declare to Grandfather. "Who knows what she'll become if she is turned loose upon the world!"

Grandfather would only smile deprecatingly at such words

and seek excuses for his favorite. At the same time, everyone in the church at the diocesan school would be listening spellbound to Katya's pure and clear voice, and this made her brothers tease her, calling her "God's little pipe organ" and making her cry. No doubt about it, Katya was a real tearaway. One of her pranks occurred when a touring opera group was staging its first open-air performance one summer in the city gardens. That evening she crept out of her bedroom and, accompanied by two of her brothers (students of a military school), climbed over some neighboring rooftops, slid down a water pipe, and sneaked into the city gardens. Sitting ticketless on a fence with the boys, she listened to the whole opera. The next day she was severely punished for the rips in her dress, but her brothers kept their mouths shut, and Grandmother did not find out how the dress came to be in such a sorry state. No doubt she would have had a heart attack if she had learned the truth.

Blessed with perfect pitch, Katya could reproduce whole arias she had heard only once even though she did not understand all the words, distorting them and even occasionally making them up as she went along. She was fascinated by the melodies and happily sang both the women's and the men's parts.

10
Enter Prince Meshchersky

At that time, a rumor flew around the district that Prince Meshchersky lay close to death in his Poltava palace. The best doctors had been summoned from Moscow and Petersburg, but the prince's heart was failing, and pneumonia was tightening its grip on his enfeebled lungs. All those who surrounded him were in despair, but then someone told them about Podborsky, the experienced and well-known district doctor. So they sent for him as a last resort. A carriage was despatched for him with, for some reason, a sealed envelope containing a large sum of money as an advance fee. Grandfather was offended and, without even opening the envelope, sent the carriage back to Vesely Podol, the palace. What was it that annoyed Grandfather most? The carriage with the Meshchersky crest and lackey outriders, followed through the town by a crowd of local urchins who had never seen such a sight in their lives? The money-filled envelope, handed to him coldly by the estate steward who had come to escort him to the prince's bedside? Or perhaps—and this is the likeliest reason—the sight of Grandmother, who fussed around oohing and aahing, fired by visions of a radical change in their fortunes, and who threatened to enact a scene of epic proportions should he refuse to seize this chance to advance himself? In any case, Grandfather found the whole situation so distasteful that he flatly refused to attend the prince. With chilling courtesy, he explained his refusal by pointing out that a man in the prince's position was already receiving the benefit of treatment by the leading lights of the Moscow and Petersburg medical world and that the advice of an ordinary district doctor like himself was hardly likely to be of use.

Grandmother succumbed to hysterics, accompanied by frenzied weeping and a stream of bitter recriminations, then retreated to her bedroom with an ice pack for her head. The day passed with the children tiptoeing around the house in order not to disturb their mother. The servant put out a cold collation, after which the children were sent to their beds.

Night fell, but the light in Grandfather's study continued to burn. His conscience bothered him, giving him no rest. Finally he decided that he had been wrong to refuse, for to a doctor every sick person should be of equal concern, be he a prince or a pauper. Having made this admission to himself, he gathered up his bag, told the servant to lock up after him, hired a passing hackney-carriage, and drove off to see the prince.

Despite his years, the prince had quite a sound constitution, and the greatest danger he faced at that time was probably the large number of doctors and physicians engaged in treating him. As was to be expected, these doctors and professors all differed in their opinions about the best treatment for their patient, and denigrated the recommendations of their colleagues, each one claiming that only the treatment prescribed by *him* was likely to save the prince's life. These quarrels would inevitably lead to the convocation of yet another panel of exerts, and the patient, in the meantime, grew steadily weaker. Podborsky examined the prince and said that he could restore the patient to health only if all the "experts" were removed, leaving him in sole charge of the treatment. The prince agreed without a moment's hesitation. The medical luminaries were paid off and left the palace in high dudgeon.

The prince's condition was very serious indeed. He had been shot through the lungs a number of times in battle, and, even when he was young, there were times when his sputum contained blood. Now he was in danger of succumbing to tuberculosis from a severe cold which had developed complications.

On Grandfather's orders, the heavy brocade hangings surrounding the prince's bed were drawn aside, and the bed itself was moved into the spacious, sunlit ballroom of the palace. To avert the buildup of fluid in the lungs, the doctor ordered his patient to sit in a large Voltaire armchair, where he was to stay all day, even if he should drop off to sleep. The nurses on duty around the clock were charged with making certain that the patient was warmly wrapped in blankets, while the fresh air streaming in through the opened windows forced him to breathe more deeply, stimulating his sluggish circulation. Through the windows, the prince could watch white-sailed skiffs dancing across the blue waters of the lake and gulls wheeling overhead. The compresses which had drained his strength were removed and regular baths substituted. The medications that had been pumped into him were gradually replaced by the homeopathic remedies Grandfather always used to treat his patients. Especially effective was an infusion of eucalyptus and agave administered in hot milk with a generous amount of mustard-flower honey—invaluable for relieving racking spasms of coughing. Grandfather's only thought was that here was a human life he had to save. He realized that his constant attendance was vital, so he sent Grandmother a note that he would remain with the prince for as long as his presence was necessary. He was very conscious of his responsibility, especially as all the other doctors had been sent away on his insistence.

After two weeks, when the prince was clearly well on the

way to recovery, Grandfather decided that it was safe for him to leave. But he encountered unexpected resistance from the prince. Doctor and patient had become great friends over those weeks and spent most evenings playing draughts or just talking.

By this time the prince already knew a great deal about his new friend, about his honesty and his scrupulous attitude about money matters; he had also heard a lot from his own servants, who had spared no effort in finding out all they could about Dr. Podborsky around the district. So now the prince was at a loss as to how he could reward the man to whom he owed his life. He would have been happy to offer the doctor a permanent position as his family physician, with a salary many times greater than the pathetic remuneration received by district doctors. However, he understood that such an offer would only give offense.

Even though Grandfather was adamant about not prolonging his stay at Vesely Podol, they parted on the best of terms. "I am sorry, Prince," he said, with a smile. "I would be delighted to remain for a while longer as your guest, but it is out of the question. I have other patients waiting for me, both old and new."

Their parting was not, however, without an awkward moment. As Podborsky had spent several weeks treating the prince, the latter took a bundle of large notes and sealed them into an envelope, which he handed directly to the doctor. It is not hard to imagine the prince's amazement when the latter, without batting an eyelash, tore open the envelope then and there, and began to count out the money. He then replaced some of the banknotes in the envelope and laid it on the frame of a large mirror in the palace vestibule.

"You have given me far too much," he said, smiling gently. "I have taken the amount due me, and the remainder is yours. You may yet have need of it."

That evening, the prince wrote in his diary, "What an extraordinary man this Prokofi Semyonovich is! It is impossible to take offense, even though his behavior is quite uncivil! However, I shall not let matters rest as they are. He saved my life, and I intend to thank him as the good friend he has become."

A few Sundays later, the legendary court carriage of the Meshcherskys, with its crests and lackeys, drew up again outside the small, one-story house in which the Podborskys lived. The prince hoped to find the whole family at home. Grandmother's feelings defy description. The prince, the prince himself, had come to visit! The drabness of her everyday life seemed suddenly transformed by this near-miracle! Fussing and panting, she rushed up to her bedroom and flung open the doors of the wardrobe housing her simple dresses. But they were clearly unsuitable to receive such an exalted guest. She hurried over to an old chest, pulled out some long unworn, old-fashioned dress reeking strongly of mothballs, and tugged it on, albeit with considerable difficulty. Grandfather stood by, biting his lips with embarrassment as she dipped and curtsied before the prince, twittering inanities in French.

Prince Meshchersky, with characteristic tact, pretended not to notice the furor caused by his arrival.

"What lovely children you have," he remarked. "How I should like to be able to do something for them."

Grandfather hastened to decline. "What for? They don't lack anything. The boys, thank God, are able to study in a military academy because of their birth. Then they'll become officers and embark on a military career. As for the girls—"

Whatever disclaimer he had been about to make on his daughters' behalf was interrupted by Katya's clear voice. "Please, Prince, take me out of the diocesan school!"

Her parents could only gasp at her forwardness, but it was too late.

"Why don't you like it there?" asked the prince.

"In the first place, because my brothers tease me and call me 'God's pipe organ,' and in the second place, because I don't like the archbishop."

"Why not?"

"Because at every liturgy he gives me communion bread."

"And what would you like?"

"Me? An orange, of course!"

"What else would you like?"

"I'd like to become a singer."

"Well, in that case, why don't you sing something for me? Anything you like!"

Katya was not disconcerted in the least. She was used to singing solo parts in church and to having an audience. Playing with her friends, she had often pretended to be a singer on stage, and now some instinct told her that this elderly and important man could do a great deal for her. Drawing breath, she began to sing everything she knew. Being little more than a child, she frequently did not understand fully the meaning of the words she was singing. Launching into Tamara's aria from Rubinstein's opera *The Demon*, she quite unself-consciously changed the stress on the words in one line, with the result that instead of singing "And you appeared," in her rendition that line became "And a honeycomb appeared." She was convinced that the heroine of the opera was singing about bees and honey. She was well into the opening of Mephistopheles's aria from *Faust* when the prince signaled her to stop and turned to her parents with unconcealed enthusiasm.

"Your daughter has a unique voice, perfect pitch, and an amazing musical memory. I feel that it is my duty to do everything possible to assist this great future singer!"

Katya's fate was sealed. Her parents did not feel that they could refuse such a generous offer, and the whole family felt absolutely bowled over. In fact, Katya was the calmest of all. When the prince prepared to leave late that evening, her father tried to elicit some sign of gratitude from her.

"Do you understand what the prince is going to do for you?" he asked her in front of everyone.

"When I become a singer," she answered with dignity, "I shall repay the prince."

Several days later Dr. Podborsky was transferred to a practice in Kiev, and the family moved into a new spacious apartment which the prince had rented for them on the Kreschatik, the main street of the city. Katya began to attend high school and in her free time commenced music lessons with teachers from the Kiev Conservatory. She learned notes, musical theory, and her first solfeggio. She was afire with the desire to learn and gave herself wholeheartedly to the world of music which was her natural element. She progressed so well not because she was particularly studious, but because this was a life she could not have dreamed of during her unhappy and cheerless childhood. The story of Cinderella was coming true to life: the general dogsbody, the least loved of her mother's daughters, now seemed to promise the family fame, wealth, and happiness! It was Katya on whom Grandmother now pinned all her hopes.

A senior student at the Kiev Conservatory, the talented young future conductor Ivan Gardinsky fell in love with Katya at first sight, and it was his most treasured ambition to conduct operas in which she would star. He introduced Katya to his parents at a concert. They were so enchanted by her that they went out of their way to meet the Podborskys, and the two families became close friends.

Katya and Ivan became engaged; she was attracted to him mainly because of their shared love of music and the theater. She gave no thought to married family life, especially since the Podborskys and the Gardinskys realized that the young couple still had some years of study before them. The young couple had to earn their happiness and establish themselves in the world of the arts. However, Ivan Gardinsky, who loved Katya passionately and jealously, insisted that their engagement be formally announced. In this, he was supported by his parents. The betrothal took place, and the young couple exchanged rings. Ivan's jealousy was appeased. Katya had pledged her troth to him before God and people, and that meant that she was his.

As for Katya, she was finding new and exciting fields in a

world that had been hitherto unknown. It was like living in a fairy tale made real by the magic touch of the elderly Prince Meshchersky. As she was one of the students receiving a stipend from the prince, she was frequently invited to participate in performances and concerts held in his Vesely Podol palace. She would spend several days at a time there, chaperoned (like most of the other girls) by her mother.

The prince, who was quite a proficient painter in oils himself, was a lover of art and had been a close friend of the artist Karl Bryulov and then the famous painter of maritime scenes Ayvazovsky, with whom he maintained a lively correspondence over many years. Next to the palace picture gallery, there was another smaller gallery which was used to exhibit the work of art students who were subsidized by the prince. Pianists and conductors from the Moscow Conservatory were often invited to the palace to accompany the performances of budding ballerinas and singers. Katya could hardly wait for the time when her teachers would consider her sufficiently advanced to take part in one of these Conservatory concerts for the first time.

Especially memorable were visits to Vesely Podol during the summer vacations. The bountiful Ukraine greeted the young people with mounds of watermelons, canteloupes, apples, pears, and cherries by the bucketful, and the succession houses of the estate offered rare treats in the form of exotic varieties of peaches, grapes, and any number of rare hybrid fruits.

The main "knights avenue" leading to the lake was lined on both sides with flowering rosebushes, and the sails of skiffs, like the unfurled wings of great white birds, glided in the distance, ever ready for a race. At night the skiffs were illuminated by colored lanterns.

The prince was a keen sportsman. He was tall and lean, with a strongly muscled, lithe body. He taught the young people fencing and horseback riding and was fond of breaking in young and particularly difficult, spirited horses.

Unlike all the other girls, Katya quickly became an outstanding horsewoman. It was as though she had been born to the saddle. She soon outstripped her contemporaries and, despite her extreme youth, was able to exhibit her prowess, eyes shining and cheeks flushed with pride of achievement. The prince, overcome with admiration, could hardly tear his eyes away from her.

How different she was from all the others! All the girls vied with each other for the prince's attention, trying to outshine each other in his eyes and win his special regard. Katya, on the other hand, was completely natural, and her genuine gaiety and high spirits were totally devoid of coquetry.

The prince had been a widower for many years and found pleasure in the company of young people. His only daughter was far away in Italy; he was generous by nature, and his wealth enabled him to act as a benefactor, receiving nothing but smiles and seeing happily flushed young faces in return. Surrounded by the talented young people he discovered and sponsored, he felt younger himself. At the same time, he was careful to treat all his youthful protégés equally, and nobody could accuse him of favoritism. He also went to great pains to be a fair and impartial judge of their achievements.

While staying at Vesely Podol, the young people were able to amuse themselves by holding boat races and swimming competitions on the lake, exercising in the gymnasium and riding, then gathering at set times of the day for breakfast, lunch, and dinner.

After a while, however, the prince found himself experiencing some new feeling he was hard put to define—or perhaps did not dare to define, even to himself. Involuntarily, he found himself watching Katya all the time, noting her every step and every word. He knew that in the middle of the night, when everyone was asleep, she would throw on her white dressing gown and creep to the very top of the palace tower, to the observatory. Once there, she would study the planets and the zodiac signs painted on the walls and make notes about that which had appealed to her imagination. Later she would copy these notes into her commonplace book. In the evenings, when the other youngsters would pass the time boating on the lake, weaving garlands or playing tag and hide-and-seek, Katya would retreat to the library, settle herself in one of the deep armchairs, and read until evening tea was served. Afterward, she invariably made her way to the room housing the porcelain collection, where she already had her favorite vases, chandeliers, and figurines: a shepherd offering a shepherdess a bouquet, a marquise alighting from a sedan chair, a couple of Italian gallants fighting a fierce duel with sabers. There were many figures of couples in love, frozen forever in a delicate turn of the minuet or immortalized in the serious moment when she hides her face with her fan and turns her head, unwilling to listen to him, while he perseveres and passes her a sealed billet-doux in a posy of flowers. Then there was a happy family group, resting in a forest glade under a large, overhanging tree: children, exhausted from running and playing, lolled in the grass, looking at their faithful friends, two golden-coated borzois who looked back at them with devotion in their eyes. A practice Katya observed every day without fail was a visit to the picture gallery; she would go early in the morning, as if to chapel, before coffee was served. First she would stand before the Botticelli Madonna and then move on to the masterpieces of other great Italian artists, whose works unfolded the birth and earthly sufferings of Christ before her discerning eyes.

Many of the art students subsidized by the prince would put up their easels around the park, painting its picturesque vistas and the shores of the lake. Knowing that the prince himself was fond of drawing, they once prevailed upon him to show them his albums of watercolors and oil paintings. Everybody was most impressed and took pains to voice approval and admiration. The prince noticed that Katya was standing a little aside and not joining in the general chorus of praise.

"You don't like them?" he asked.

"I suppose I'm not really qualified to judge," she replied seriously. "Until now, I have always admired everything that you do . . . But if I were you, I would not paint."

"Why is that?"

"Well, if only because you have the priceless canvases of world-famous artists before your eyes in your collection. You see them every day, and such a comparison is the worst criticism possible of your work."

Everyone was horrified by Katya's impertinence, except the prince.

"You see," he said with a kindly smile, "I know that in art I am as much a dilettante as in many other things. I realize that God has not endowed me with the gift of being a great artist. But what can I do? I enjoy playing the piano. I love to sing and write. And although I know that I do all these things badly, they still bring me pleasure."

Probably it was from this day that he valued and loved Katya even more. She had been a mere adolescent when he met her, but now she was growing into young womanhood, completing secondary education, and preparing to enter the Conservatory. Her teachers confidently predicted a brilliant future for her.

And what about Katya herself? Her first attachment and love in life had been her father, and now the prince had an equal place in her heart. She did not even perceive him as a person, but as some kind of magic figure, a spirit of good and light, and she never ceased to wonder how he took the trouble to ensure the education of so many young people, how he watched the progress of each and every one of his protégés, how he was upset by lack of progress or sincerely delighted by their every achievement. With every year, Katya grew increasingly attached to her father's friend.

At the same time, a frightful family drama occurred in the Podborsky household. The oldest daughter, Olga, who had been engaged for some time to a young professor of philosophy, took advantage of the absence of her mother and her fiancé's parents—who had gone to Petersburg to pick up her wedding dress, veil, and wedding presents—to break into Grandfather's desk, remove her passport, and elope with a passing cuirassier officer, Alexei Bodnevsky. Even though they married, the elopement caused a scandal that was impossible to suppress. This action by her favorite daughter was a terrible blow to Grandmother, and her heart began to act up. The family beauty, Anatolia, did not give much cause for optimism, either, with her difficult and carping nature. All the money that had been squandered on her drawing, dancing, music, and singing lessons had not brought about the desired results, but merely proved the mediocrity of her abilities. She did have an attractive, strong soprano, but as she was tone deaf, her voice was not much of an asset. The only hope was Katya, and Grandmother, with typical Polish vainglory, began to take a great pride in her middle daughter, who henceforth became the object of all her hopes and trust.

In the meantime, Katya was encountering a number of disappointments, and these were all due to the prince. His attitude toward her became very inconsistent. He blew hot and cold, first singling her out for attention and then for no obvious reason becoming cold and distant, occasionally even harsh. There was no way she could know that he was undergoing an inward struggle, that he thought of his feelings for her as indecent and almost blasphemous. So he exerted all his willpower to quell the emotions which seared his heart like a raging flame. He kept reminding himself that he had three granddaughters in Italy, the eldest of whom was the same age as Katya.

When Katya completed her secondary schooling, the prince despatched her, with her mother, to the Moscow Philharmonic. They lived quietly in furnished rooms, and the prince would visit them from time to time when he came to Moscow on business.

During those years, the friendship between the prince and Grandfather grew and deepened. Despite the fact that Grandfather was a true democrat at heart and was very sensitive in all matters concerning money, he nevertheless saw what a key role the prince was playing in his favorite daughter's life and therefore raised no objections to accepting the prince's plan of sending Katya to the Moscow Philharmonic.

Katya's fiancé, however, took a radically different view of the matter. For him this was the beginning of a future tragedy. He had felt for some time that Katya was drawing further and further away from him. It was almost as though he no longer existed for her. Who, he asked himself, was weaning Katya's affections away from him? Burning with jealousy, he began to try to determine the unknown usurper, but despite all his vigilance he could not see any likely rival around his fiancée.

The Gardinsky parents took umbrage on their only son's behalf and were highly critical of Katya.

"She can't really love him if she doesn't miss him and makes no effort to see him," they reasoned. "First she studies one thing, then another, then she goes off to the prince's palace to sing and enjoy herself yet never has any free time for her fiancé or for us, her future in-laws!"

But Ivan Gardinsky sensed some deeper, hidden reason for the change in his fiancée. "His Katya" seemed to have disappeared, to be replaced by a stranger.

Nowadays Katya only came home to Kiev for Christmas and Easter and during her summer vacation, half of which she spent with her mother at Vesely Podol.

"It is so long since we saw each other," Ivan would say to Katya every time they met. "I miss you so terribly! But what about you? Do you miss me at least a little?"

"Of course I do," Katya would respond, trying to smile, yet looking anywhere but at him. She would pointedly avoid discussing any details concerning their future married life, any plans at all.

"We can't go on like this," said Gardinsky when the time came for Katya to return to Moscow yet again. "If you don't marry me straightaway, that means you don't love me. Surely there is no need to wait until you finish studying at the Philharmonic?"

Katya paled: she had been expecting, yet dreading, such an ultimatum for quite a while.

Grandfather, who was present, came to his daughter's rescue. "Vanya!" he chided. "Remember our agreement. Katya must complete her education, and you have no right to deny her that. It's impossible for a married woman to devote the necessary time and attention to serious studies. For that matter, you have not yet conducted at a single ballet, a single opera, and you are in no position to support a family. It would be madness for you to marry now, because it would mean abandoning your studies and directing all your energies toward setting up a household!"

So poor Gardinsky said good-bye to Katya without receiving a direct answer from her.

And Katya, who was not yet able to admit even to herself that she loved another, silently vowed never to marry at all. She would devote her entire life to her art. Running away from her own emotions, she managed to convince herself that she did not love Vanya only because she was not capable of loving anyone, ever. His passion, his jealousy, and his impatience to make her his wife frightened and even repelled her. She began to hate him. Marriage? A ring on her finger, which would bind her as surely as a chain for the rest of her life? Then there might be a child . . . or more than one . . . and that's happiness? To go on stage, pregnant, and try to act the role of fifteen-year-old Juliet? What a nightmare! And at home—diapers, washing, children's ailments . . . was it for this that she had spent years of study, and would spend even more? What about her dreams of going to Italy, seeing the blue waters of the Mediterranean, Milan, the immortal Italian opera . . . and perhaps even making a concert tour around the world?

A vision of the prince's cool, calm face rose unbidden in her mind, his unruffled composure, which was belied only by the glint in his intelligent, gray-blue eyes every time he kissed her hand and pronounced, "Katya, you have immense talent! The day will come when the whole world shall listen to you with bated breath, and I shall do everything I can to bring it about!"

The summer before graduation from the Philharmonic was spent, as usual, in Kiev. Katya's graduation concert was the main topic of conversation in the Podborsky household. She would be singing scenes from *Romeo and Juliet* for her final assessment. Romeo's part would be sung by Leonid Vitalyevich Sobinov, a fellow student under Professor Bezhevich. Gardinsky visited the Podborsky house almost daily, still hoping against hope, even though in his heart he realized it was not just her singing that stole Katya from him, but also the prince, with his wealth and opportunities to interfere in Katya's life. So when Katya calmly and seriously asked him to forgive her for her immature mistake and to release her from an engagement which could not lead to the altar, Gardinsky blamed the prince. He was beside himself, but none of his pleas, not even his tears, changed Katya's resolve. The attempts made by Gardinsky's parents to persuade Katya to think again were just as fruitless. Grandmother and Grandfather, who could not help feeling somewhat guilty about the Gardinskys, also tried to influence Katya to change her mind. This served only to infuriate her. She would turn pale, her eyes would burn with a kind of fanatic fervor, and she would reiterate, "I shall never, ever, marry anyone! I would rather die!"

She refused to see her fiancé one last time and sent back his ring through a third party before returning to Moscow for her final year at the Philharmonic.

Gardinsky was frantic with grief and the desire for revenge. He found a printer in Kiev who for a large sum of money agreed to do a rush job. The order was to make an enlargement of one of Katya's best portraits and, under it, in large letters, print the following text:

PRINCE MESHCHERSKY'S NEW VICTIM!
THE LATEST MISTRESS OF
THAT OLD MAECENAS AND LECHER!!!

Hundreds of these posters were printed and appeared overnight on all the main thoroughfares and public places of Kiev.

Not long before this, the prince had been the marshal of the Poltava nobility, but at this time he had been elevated to marshal of the nobility in Moscow, so he was a very well-known figure indeed.

On the same day, the police came to arrest Gardinsky, but they were too late. He had shot himself.

The shadow of her former fiancé's suicide darkened Katya's happy young life with her first experience of mourning. But that was not all; malicious gossip was already linking her name with the prince's. Suddenly it occurred to Katya that her position and that of her mother were indeed ambiguous. It was as though the scales had suddenly fallen from her eyes. Indisputably the prince had gone far beyond his normal degree of patronage in his dealings with her. There were those who took a charitable view of the situation, pointing out that Podborsky had once saved the prince from certain death and that this was the reason for the friendship and extraordinary degree of attention offered by the prince. But the world at large is cruel and tends to ignore that which is good and virtuous, preferring the bad and the compromising. The tide of gossip and innuendo made Katya see many recent developments in an entirely different light. She began to understand the change in the prince and his real feelings for her. Trying to suppress these alarming insights, she had to admit fearfully to herself that this old man, this friend of her father's, had become the most important person in her life.

Katya seemed to mature overnight. She was restrained in her dealings with the prince, and there was no trace left of her former gaiety. She retreated into herself. The shade of her dead fiancé seemed to stand between her and the prince like a silent, ever-present reproach. She remembered the times when she was a child that the prince would hug her, stroke her hair, and kiss her cheek. Now he was cool, aloof, and tended to look past her in conversation, as though unwilling to meet her eyes. They met less frequently, too, even though Katya and Grandmother rarely left Moscow in those days. Kiev was still buzzing with gossip about the Podborskys, about Katya, and about her fiancé's suicide. The business with the leaflets, which had been stuck up all over the city, had compromised her reputation considerably.

But if Grandmother vacillated between indignation and despair about the slurs on her daughter's reputation, Katya herself was preoccupied by completely different thoughts. Could it be? Could it be, she asked herself, that the prince shares my emotions? Am I mistaken in thinking that he is finding it harder and harder to suppress his feelings for me? But what would such an erudite, unusual man see in someone like her? What was she to him? Could it be that Vanya had been right, and she was just a fleeting fancy, a new toy?

On the day of Katya's graduation, she and Grandmother were invited to a celebration dinner at the prince's large, white-columned town residence on the corner of Tverskaya Street and Degtyarny Lane, where the Minsk Hotel stands today. As usual there were to be many guests, but the prince had asked that Katya and her mother come a little earlier.

He received them in his study. He kissed Grandmother's hand in greeting and congratulated her on her daughter's brilliant success. He then raised Katya's hand to his lips, too, saying smilingly that this was in order now that she was an adult. Then he opened a drawer in his desk and took out a long jeweler's box. A beautiful gold bracelet studded with diamonds and sapphires sparkled on a bed of black velvet.

"Your voice will earn you many valuable gifts," said the prince. "But I hope that this bracelet will always be particularly dear to you, because it was the first present given to you as you stood on the threshold of fame."

Barely managing to contain her delight, Grandmother hastened to fasten the glittering bracelet around her daughter's wrist. Katya thanked the prince and automatically curtsied to him, but he put out a restraining hand.

"Let that be your last curtsy," he smiled. "You must leave all such childish actions behind you now, for not only are you grown up, but you are a singer."

He spoke jokingly, and Katya stood before him, her eyes lowered in sadness. In that moment, Ivan Gardinsky's face seemed to rise before her . . . Vanya! . . . How delighted he would have been to attend her graduation performance, how happy he would have been to be the first to run up to the stage and congratulate her! Who better than he would have been able to choose the opera in which she would sing a leading role for the first time? Had it not been his most cherished dream to conduct the opera in which she would make her debut? It was at this time that their joint creative life should have started! And what right did she have to be in love with the prince, an elderly man who had fulfilled an obligation to her father by affording one of his children the opportunity to gain a full education? Such were the thoughts running through Katya's head as she stood before the prince in silence while he maintained a lively conversation with her mother. Then a lackey entered and announced that the first guests had arrived. The prince left to receive his guests, and there followed a dinner lasting many hours.

Before the tea tray was brought in, the guests wandered off, some to play cards, some to the music room; others gathered in the drawing room in small groups to chat. Although all the windows were open, it was sultry and close, so Katya and the prince went out onto the balcony for a breath of fresh air.

Unexpectedly he put his arms around her and would have drawn her to him, but she slipped out of his hold. Burning with indignation, she tore the bracelet he had given her from her wrist and slashed him across the face with its heavy chain. Every drop of color drained out of his face, and he bowed silently. He remained standing there as she turned and ran back inside. The blood seemed to pound in her veins: it had come, that yearned-for moment when the prince showed his true feelings for her. It seemed, though, that he thought to make her his mistress. Gardinsky must have been right! After all, it was not an unusual occurrence for members of high society to take actresses, ballerinas, or singers as mistresses. Moreover, she was under a great obligation to him, and obligations must be repaid. . . .

She found Grandmother, an ardent cardplayer, totally immersed in a rubber of bridge. She touched her lightly on the shoulder and bent to murmur in her ear, "I feel unwell. I've got a blinding migraine. Please, let's go home!"

"Home?" repeated Grandmother, looking at Katya's burning cheeks in astonishment. "What on earth is the matter with you? Well, what is it?" she repeated in the face of her daughter's silence. "And where's the prince? Didn't you go out on the terrace together?"

"He has excused me . . . I've already said my good-byes. Please, no more questions! We must leave immediately. . . ."

"What about the carriage?" objected Grandmother, who by this time had become accustomed to being picked up and driven home in the prince's carriage. "And what's more, I can hardly go rushing off without taking my leave of the prince!"

"We'll stop a hackney-carriage!" Katya threw over her shoulder, heading for the door and leaving Grandmother no choice but to follow her as discreetly as possible.

It was not until they were on their way in a hired carriage that Grandmother noticed the bracelet given to Katya by the prince was missing.

"What happened to it?" she asked, alarmed. "Don't tell me you've lost it?"

For the first time in her life, Katya refused to answer a

question from her mother. She leaned back against the cushions and looked back at her mother silently and coldly, discouraging any further queries.

Early the following morning, one of the prince's servants came to the lodgings Katya and her mother had in Merzlyakovsky Lane. Presenting the prince's compliments, the servant handed Katya a package, "with something you lost in his house yesterday." The package contained a jeweler's box, which Katya recognized immediately. In it, lay the same bracelet, on the clasp of which, engraved in tiny letters, were the words: "Unexpectedly and forever."

The prince must have ordered this message engraved after Katya and Grandmother left so hurriedly the previous evening, and the jeweler had had to do it during the night. Grandmother smiled, but shook her head perplexedly as she read and reread the engraved words. Katya did her best to look surprised, although her heart had already deciphered the meaning behind those three words: this was the prince's declaration of love. Their meeting had been an unexpected event in the prince's life, but it would remain in his heart forever.

Toward evening on the same day, the prince came to see the Podborskys without warning or invitation. Kissing Grandmother's hands one after the other, he offered his apologies for such a lapse of manners.

"My house is always full of guests, and it is impossible for us to sit down and have a quiet discussion on matters of real importance," he said apologetically. "The fact that Katya has successfully completed the Philharmonic is just the first step toward becoming a singer. Of course, I have the connections and the means to enable Katya, with her voice, to be taken on at the Bolshoi Theater, but I think this would be a mistake. In the first place, Katya is still little more than a child and must acquire social confidence. Her exceptional modesty inhibits her movements on stage; she needs training and professional deportment. Although she sang faultlessly at her graduation performance, she is so unsure of herself that it reflects on her bearing on stage, occasionally making her seem awkward. She needs polishing, like a precious stone. She must still master the art of acting. As she performs different operatic parts, they will hone her talent. It is not enough for her to study under one teacher," he concluded decisively. "So there's no need for you to stay on in Moscow any longer. Go back to Prokofi Semyonovich in Kiev and ask him whether he will give his consent for you to go abroad, not just for a brief stay but for several years. To go to Italy, where Katya will be able to perfect her artistry."

Katya did not sleep a wink that night. Her mind was in turmoil. How, she asked herself, how could she, a very young woman, have dared to strike an elderly man, her father's friend, who had been a benefactor not just to her family, but to so many talented young people? Youngsters who loved and respected him? And she, who had dared to insult him, was repaid by yet another gesture of kindness! She was deservedly shamed by his generosity, and at the same time she had to face a whole flood of new ideas and feelings. Clearly, by sending her to Italy for some years, he was prepared to lose her once she left his immediate sphere of influence. A new life, new friends, new encounters would surely contribute to this. The prince would be fully aware of this and, with typical self-sacrifice, almost seemed to be in a hurry to give her her freedom and tear her out of his heart. . . . And what of her unforgivable action in flinging his gift back in his face?! Yet it was motivated only by a suddenly awakened feeling of outraged feminine pride. How often had he kissed her over the years? Indeed, how often had she flung herself into his arms to thank him for some act of kindness or other? She had always treated his caresses as those of her father, but on this occasion . . . ? It was as though she had suddenly awakened and taken fright at herself. She was fully aware that the man with whom she was in love was some years older than her own father. Yet love him she did, more than anyone in the world! The projected trip to Italy made her feel more apprehension than pleasure. How would she live without seeing him? Surely he, too, would feel sad and lonely; he was old and could die at any time. Just this thought was enough to make her blood run cold and all joy fade from life.

The bracelet was back on her wrist, and her heart seemed to beat faster every time she looked at it, seeming to repeat, "forever. . . . forever . . . forever . . ."

And so Grandmother and Katya returned to Kiev. The Podborsky family, with typical tempestuous Polish temperament, greeted them with boisterous pleasure. The moment she had crossed the threshold, Grandmother—while exchanging hugs and kisses with everyone—launched into a breathless account of the prince's plans to send her and Katya to Italy. The joy on Grandfather's face was replaced by sadness. Grandfather had missed his favorite daughter greatly and did not welcome the prospect of a new and lengthy separation. Furthermore, as the old saying goes, "A house without a mistress is like an orphan." Anatolia hated housework, had been lazy from childhood, and the hired housekeeper was no real substitute for a proper mistress in the home.

"This is a serious matter, and one that can't be resolved here in the hallway," said Grandfather. "Go and clean up after your journey, and I'll order dinner to be served."

Nevertheless the main topic of discussion over dinner, and later over the teacups, was the prince's offer.

"Why is it so essential to go abroad?" demanded Grandfather eventually, with distinct annoyance. "There are any number of famous singers who have managed perfectly well without going overseas for training. Surely Katya could sing for a while here, in Russia? She has her whole life in front of her; there's plenty of time to go abroad later!"

He realized, however, that his objections really arose from his reluctance to be parted again from his wife and daughter. He also realized the scope of the opportunity being offered to Katya and he knew that the prince was getting on in years. So, finally, he gave his consent, albeit with a heavy heart. Two weeks later, a telegram arrived from the prince in Moscow inquiring whether Grandfather had given his permission for his wife and daughter to go to Italy. The same telegram invited them to come to Vesely Podol for a fortnight of graduation concerts at which all the students he had sponsored would show their talents before setting out on their chosen careers.

The occasion turned out to be particularly interesting since the young graduates were all very different. A student who had completed the Stroganov Art School brought along some of the oil paintings he had submitted for his final examinations, and one of them was a very good portrait of Prince Meshchersky. Two ballerinas who had just graduated from the School of Choreography brought their partners to give an exhibition performance. The music was provided by a trio from the Moscow Conservatory. The cellist in this trio later gave several solo performances, as he had just graduated as a player of that instrument from the Conservatory. At these exhibition-performance evenings, musical accompaniment was usually provided by the same pianists who had come from Moscow on the prince's invitation, and then became regular visitors to Vesely Podol. So all such gatherings were like a meeting of close friends, and the atmosphere could not have been more warm and informal. The young people would dine al fresco and, ignoring the tempting offerings concocted by vying chefs, would pile their plates high with golden cobs of corn wrapped in starched napkins and smothered in melted butter to delight the palate.

The gymnasium room stood empty; foils and sabers lay forgotten. Skiffs, waving colored flags in the breeze, remained idly at their moorings. The neighing of horses, who pawed the earth in their stalls and called to their erstwhile riders, went unheard. The prince and his guests would climb into carts filled with fragrant straw and, equipped with samovars and huge picnic baskets, drive out to the woods from morning until evening to look for mushrooms. The palace lay quiet and virtually deserted.

Two weeks flew by almost unnoticed. The exhibition concerts were repeated twice, and the last one was attended by the owners of neighboring estates. When the day of departure approached, the prince was moved to tears. On the last evening, he gathered all his protégés in one of the most exquisite salons of the palace, the Elizabethan drawing room.

"You have all brought me so much pleasure," he told them, "that I would like to ask each of you to choose, as a memento, anything you wish from my palace."

Such a tempting offer could not be refused, and the young people scattered throughout the palace to choose their gifts. Only Katya made no move to follow.

"What about you, Katya?" asked the prince gently. "Why are you standing there looking so serious?"

"Because you will not be able to give me that which I would like," she replied.

"You cannot know me very well if you doubt my word," said the prince. "What have you chosen?"

Silently she indicated a life-size portrait of the prince hanging in its oval frame in the corner of the room.

"What on earth would you want with that?" he asked in amazement. "You're going abroad, so you wouldn't even see it!"

"What of it?" she countered. "I'll take it with me everywhere. I'll have it with me instead of you," she added quietly. "I might not miss you quite as much then . . ."

That evening Katya gave the prince a photograph of herself, which I still have. By the look of it, it was taken just for him prior to her departure. There is a great deal of sweet ingenuity in her young, thin face, in her bearing and delicate figure. The serious, almost sad expression in her eyes is at sharp variance with the coquettish pose, fan in hand, dictated by the photographer. A poem is written on the back of this photograph in

Mother's hand. I have no idea whose poem it is, but its aim is clear. It is Katya's admission of love.

> There are emotions which cannot be measured
> By clarity of mind or by the spoken word
> And to acknowledge them is just as fearsome,
> For they inhabit hearts and dreams and souls.
> The heart conceals them in a jealous fastness
> As if some treasure, counter reason's voice;
> Their beauty lies in their complete concealment
> Away from scrutiny by prying eyes
> But comes a day, when through a veil of mystery
> A flash of truth illuminates the mind
> And the once-hidden feeling, like a clap of thunder,
> Triumphantly peals forth the loved one's name.
> And then? What then? Oh, then no hesitation,
> The choice is clear, and soon and close,
> Bright love, embraced with heart's rejoicing,
> Or black despair, and separation's curse . . .
>
> (VESELY PODOL, 8 September 1893)

And now, in answering the prince's question, she had given herself away, so brazenly and improperly. . . . Luckily all the other young people were too busy running from room to room in search of suitable souvenirs, or they would have been bound to interpret her behavior as a shameless attempt to ingratiate herself with their patron.

The prince showed no outward sign of surprise at Katya's explanation. Yet the portrait was packed in special securing frames and crated for transportation. I recall that we had a lot of these adjustable securing frames, which were used whenever any of our paintings were loaned out for exhibitions. Unfortunately I do not remember the name of the artist of that particular portrait, but I don't think it was by anyone prominent or I would not have forgotten. Nevertheless, in our family that paint-

ing was a favorite. It did not depict Father in his general's uniform with all his medals, nor did it show him in the magnificence
of his gold-embroidered uniform of master of horse of the imperial court. This life-size portrait, in a massive oval gold frame,
showed Father wearing a sober black civilian suit, with a black
neckcloth against a starched snow-white shirtfront. A large white
pearl pin nestled in the folds of the neckcloth.

11
Katya, Maestro Bimboni, and La Scala

And so, Grandmother and Katya set off from Russia. Katya's youth, and her encounter with new people and places, had predictable results. The past receded in favor of an exciting present. In Italy, Katya felt as though she had found a second home. Somehow every new town seemed familiar and the Italians, as though they were her own people. Their language, with its rich music, emotion, and mimicry, attracted her immediately, and she was quick to pick it up. Wandering around the streets, the waterfronts, and the marketplaces, she absorbed its nuances and intonations, studied the gestures of the speakers, and was soon speaking Italian as fluently as a native, much to the dismay of Grandmother, who considered the "common mannerisms and gestures" of the Italians as verging on the indecent.

The days flew by, then the months, but Katya changed and matured as though years were passing. Suddenly she flowered into a real beauty: slim, of medium height, with heavy waves of chestnut hair shot with golden glints over a delicate face with flawless features. Her eyes were a deep, velvety brown. Her fair skin flushed easily; she was a vital, vibrant personality who threw herself into everything she did with wholehearted dedication. But the most eye-catching feature of her face was her mouth, and the dimples every smile brought to its corners, exposing beautiful, even, white teeth. Katya's beauty was a cause for great concern to Grandmother. There were floods of letters from admirers, serenades under their windows; sometimes they were even mobbed in the streets. Yet despite all her vivacity and love of life, Katya remained impervious to the attention she attracted. It's as though she is under some spell, thought Grandmother, perplexed.

Katya had three instructors: one worked with her on vocals; the other taught her stagecraft; and the third dealt only with coloratura and trills. Italy rekindled Katya's burning desire to learn and achieve her most treasured goal, so she immersed herself totally in the unremitting regime that is the lot of all those who dedicate themselves to art. Katya would rise at six o'clock in the morning, go for a dip in the sea, do some exercises, and then buckle down to the day's studies, stopping only for meals and occasional short breaks. She spent her evenings with her mother, sightseeing, or, more frequently, going to the opera or some concert. As a child dreaming of becoming a singer, she had no inhibitions about singing in front of anyone willing to listen, but now the more she learned and the more famous singers she heard, the more she began to feel inadequate.

Meanwhile, in far-off Russia, there beat two concerned and loving hearts. Grandfather worried about his favorite daughter, for a singer's career is one that cannot but give rise to misgivings in a parent. The other heart belonged to the prince, who kept careful track of his beloved's progress. When Grandmother and Katya boarded the train on the first leg of their journey abroad, two experienced agents hired by the prince were in another carriage. They took lodgings not far from Grandmother and Katya, somewhere in the same street, and shadowed both ladies every time they went out. Every second day they telegraphed reports to the prince and periodically submitted detailed written reports.

But even this was not enough for the prince. It emerged later that he traveled periodically to Italy and stayed under an assumed name in one of the leading hotels. A year went by, then another, and the prince knew beyond any doubt that Katya was leading a faultless life. Every month Grandmother would receive a draft from a Moscow bank, always in the same sum, to cover their living expenses. In fairness to Grandmother, it should be noted that she always tried to be economical with these funds, and Katya herself kept a record of daily expenses, saying, "The day will come when I shall faithfully repay the prince every penny he spent on us." Therefore, the Podborsky ladies rented a small three-room apartment with a balcony on one of those winding, typically Italian, narrow streets, where you can talk to the people on the balcony opposite without raising your voice and stretch clotheslines from one building to another.

The prince sincerely regretted the situation, but he could do nothing about it without admitting that he knew every detail of their lives. He could grant himself only one indulgence. Every time he came over from Russia, he would send Katya a bouquet of roses by messenger. But Katya, thinking that they were from some unknown and unwanted admirer, invariably threw them over the balcony into the street, to the joy of the children playing below. One circumstance, however, made her wonder a little. The roses were very expensive ones and invariably the kind known as Gloire de Dijon. Moreover, they came at irregular intervals, sometimes very long ones. The secret became known only much later. When Katya was already married to the prince, he once gave her a small oil painting in a gold frame. The painting was of those very pale yellow roses which she used to receive so mysteriously when she was studying in Italy.

The time came when Katya's instructors informed her that they all felt it was time for her to test herself by appearing in a small concert. The success of this first effort exceeded all expectations. Now she had a number of prominent Italians at her feet. One of them was the fabulously rich Marquis Geomerello Ficci, who immediately held a fete in honor of the young singer at his castle. Grandmother was to recall in later years how tables laden with food were mechanically lifted to the second floor of the castle. In two or three days the marquis was already asking for Katya's hand in marriage. His proposal was declined, but he continued to hope. Celebrations in honor of the young singer continued, and Grandmother and Katya were invited to his castle again. This time, the invitation was extended to Katya's three instructors. As they sat over dessert on the suspended verandah which had been built above a lake in the grounds of the castle, listening to the splashing of fountains amid flower beds and admiring the dazzling fireworks display arranged by the marquis, the latter launched into an impassioned speech. He said that Katya's voice had conquered him and proceeded to unfold extravagant schemes for the future, which included building an opera house just for her, drawing her teachers into these plans as he obviously saw them as potential allies to his cause. Grandmother was quite overwhelmed and looked at her daughter with imploring eyes, but Katya was polite yet resolute in refusing the marquis again. (I have a vivid recollection of this middle-aged man, dressed in an embroidered jacket, black-eyed, and bewhiskered. His photograph, with a passionate dedication, was the first one in an album of admirers of Mama's voice in Italy.)

But the time for decision was drawing near. Katya was preparing to sing Michaela in *Carmen* and the leading role in *Tosca*. She and Grandmother were getting ready to travel to Milan, so that Mama could make her debut at the famous La Scala, where so many of the world's greatest singers had begun their careers. Only after the appearance at La Scala would Katya's musical career be truly launched. Before making her debut in Milan, however, Katya decided to test herself by doing a small concert tour around several of the seaside towns. She also gave a farewell concert in the town where she had lived so happily for three years, and which she had come to love.

After the thunderous applause had finally died down, Katya was approached in the wings by a young, handsome Italian. He expressed his admiration for her singing and introduced himself. Katya did not catch his name, but, as he raised her hand to his lips, he added proudly and distinctly, *"Sono Siciliano!"* ("I am a Sicilian"). Katya was rather surprised by this turn of phrase but attributed no special significance to it. One of her teachers, who happened to be standing nearby, whispered to her that she should be very careful, as the Sicilians were a very proud, fiery, and willful race. In a fit of jealousy, they would "mark" a woman, in other words, cut her face with a special knife that would leave a scar with a ragged edge. At the least suspicion of an affront, they reach for their knives. For that reason, on first acquaintance, after the customary introduction, they add the cautionary words, *"Sono Siciliano,"* as a warning. "Be careful in your dealings with me, I am Sicilian!" But Katya did not go into the implications of her teacher's warning and promptly put it out of her mind.

Cheering music lovers followed Grandmother and Katya back to their lodgings and refused to disperse. When the two ladies reemerged to climb into the hired carriage that was to take them to their boat, the adoring crowd of expansive, impulsive Italians unharnessed the horses and pulled the carriage to the docks themselves.

The boat was to sail at night. The sea was rough, heralding a storm, but the travelers were undaunted. The contract for the concert tour had been signed, and the advance fee was already in Grandmother's bag. They had to go at all costs. The wind continued to rise, and the ship pitched strongly, even though it was still at anchor. The ladies went through to their cabin, but Katya, still riding high on the wave of excitement from her performance, persuaded Grandmother to go to the restaurant. The ship was about to weigh anchor, and such moments are always exhilarating. Because of the weather, there was nobody up on deck; all the passengers had repaired to the restaurant. That is where Katya wanted to go, too, to have a look at the ladies' evening dresses, listen to the orchestra, have dinner. What could be more boring than being stuck in one's cabin? Grandmother was only too glad to accede to Katya's wishes. They redid their hair, put on their best evening dresses, and after a last critical look in the mirror proceeded to the restaurant. A wave of music and delicious odors engulfed them as they entered, the smell of the most expensive cigarettes and cigars, exclusive perfumes. . . . For a moment, it all went to Katya's head like a sip of golden, sparkling champagne. So this was that as yet unknown life, full of burning secrets and wonders, a life on the threshold of which she now stood.

The chief steward hurried forward to meet them and ushered them to a table, but as soon as they had taken their seats they saw a young Italian advancing purposefully toward them, that very same Italian who had qualified himself as a Sicilian. He greeted them punctiliously and indicated the two empty chairs at their table, obviously hoping to join the two ladies. His behavior was perfectly correct, but at the same time there was a persistent and inexplicable familiarity in his manner, so much so that the steward obviously decided this was a close friend and pulled out a chair for him.

Grandmother could only stare in amazement, but Katya, who was equally at a loss, naively asked what chance had brought the young man to the same ship.

"It was no chance, Signorina Caterina," replied the Sicilian, "but the hope with which you endowed me!"

"*Hope?* What hope?" asked Grandmother with deep foreboding.

"When your daughter and I parted, she shook my hand and said, '*Arrivederci,*' that is, until we meet again, and not '*Addio,* good-bye. Therefore, it is my right to see her again and be her escort. She has brought me great joy by giving me this hope!"

Just at that time the anchor was raised and the ship began moving away from the dock amid shouted commands, whistles and cries of farewell. Without touching the food set before them and muttering lame excuses about a sudden headache, both ladies quickly left the restaurant and hurried back to their cabin. They realized that they had fallen into a trap of some kind, that this was no joke, and that they were alone and unprotected. Grandmother rang for a maid and sent a message to the captain, asking him to come to see her on a matter of extreme urgency. Some fifteen minutes later he appeared, an elderly, very pleasant Englishman. Having heard them out, he thought deeply for a few moments, automatically pulling out a traditional captain's pipe from his pocket. However, recollecting that he was in a ladies' cabin, he put it back again without lighting it and gave his assessment of the situation.

"Yes, these Sicilians are crazy about Russian women, and your daughter is a rising singer and very beautiful to boot. Among the Sicilians, even if you leave aside their temperament, this sort of thing—if you will excuse my plain speaking—is looked upon almost as a sport. If he has set his sights on your daughter, there can be no amicable parting. I've seen such things many times in my years at sea. However, it is my duty to do everything I can to help you get out of your predicament. There is only one way out, as far as I can see, but I don't know whether you will agree to run the risks involved. I will give you three of my crew, and you will immediately leave the ship in one of the lifeboats. We are still quite close to land. But you will have to hurry. The wind is still rising, and every minute counts. We'll cover a lot of distance overnight, and it will be too late for that hotheaded young Sicilian to do anything about it by the time he discovers that you're no longer on board. I shall do everything I can to make it seem that you are both unwell and confined to your cabin. The maids will go in and out at regular intervals with morning coffee, with luncheon trays . . . Well, what do you say? Are you game?"

He received fervent assurances that they were and thanks for his help.

"Oh, I almost forgot!" added the captain. "All your luggage will naturally have to stay on the ship. I shall have it unloaded in our next port of call and left for collection. Don't worry about it. But now our concern is to save you. Put all your documents, money, checkbook, and valuables in a rubber pouch and sew it up. Then tie a cord around it and put it around your neck, under your clothes. But hurry, hurry! Time is moving on!"

In feverish haste, Grandmother and Katya began to make their preparations. In the meantime, the storm grew stronger. There was even a moment when the captain, flinging open the door of their cabin without knocking, declared, "It's too late . . . too late to leave the ship . . . the danger is too great!" But both ladies entreated him tearfully to let them proceed, promising large sums of money as reward to the sailors who would accompany them. They were not afraid, they insisted; honor was dearer to them than anything else. Any unpleasantness arising from the Sicilian's pursuit of Katya could result in a scandal. It would inevitably find its way into the newspapers and besmirch Katya's name, which was only just becoming known.

So the Podborskys' luggage remained on board the ship, including the portrait of the prince, which went with them everywhere. Both women were placed into waterproofed sacks and lashed to the lifeboat's mast, to stop them from being swept overboard. Three brawny sailors, the best swimmers and oarsmen from among the crew, set forth into the open sea. Land was still comparatively close, the sailors knew their business, but the wind roared and the waves lashed, throwing the small boat around like a matchstick. Huge walls of water loomed out of the dark and crashed down on them with incredible force, pulling them under. Then, by a lucky chance, one wave propelled them an enormous distance, right up to the shore, where it dumped the boat upside down and then began to suck it back into the deep. If both women had not been cocooned in waterproof sacks (made for just such purposes), they would have drowned, and if they had not been lashed to the sloop with ropes, they would have been swept away. But the courage, strength, and ability of the sailors saved them from certain death.

This unexpected and unfortunate flight was to cost the two women dearly: first, they both contracted heavy colds; and second, they had to pay a large cancellation fee for the planned concert tour, which naturally fell through. After they recovered from their colds and fears, Katya and Grandmother traveled to Milan to prepare for Katya's operatic debut.

To sing at La Scala is the dream of every opera singer in the world! Oh, Italy! Under your skies was born a school of singing unsurpassed elsewhere. It is further unparalleled because even those singers who have won recognition in their native land still come to you to hone their talent to perfection, to learn from your supreme school.

It is not hard to imagine with what trepidation Katya first stepped across the threshold of the Milan Opera! Back in the days of my grandparents and great grandparents it was said that, whenever a singer made his or her debut in the opera, the temperamental Italians—all of whom are connoisseurs of music—would shower the artist with either flowers or rotten fruit (which they always brought along in abundance), to show their approbation or their rejection of the singer. This may sound anecdotal now, but in those far-off days the first performance would set the future career of a singer. The new, young Russian singer was virtually an unknown; relatively few had heard her concerts or seen her name mentioned in the popular press.

It should be noted that on the night when Katya and her mother fled the ship with the help of the captain and his brave sailors, not only the women's luggage and the portrait of the prince had been left behind on the ship but also the two agents hired by the Prince. Having lost track of the two Podborskys, the agents were at a loss as to what they should do next. They had no choice but to write to the prince and admit their failure.

The prince replied with a telegram summoning both back to Russia, where he summarily dismissed them. He immediately hired two new young agents and sent them off posthaste to Milan, armed with numerous photographs of the ladies.

At last the long-awaited and frightening day of Katya's opera debut arrived. The opera being performed at La Scala was *Carmen*. The lead role was being sung by a famous Spanish singer. From the very first rehearsals, she treated the young Russian girl with a purely Latin, burning disdain. This made things very difficult and worrying for young Katya, who was still uncertain of herself and her voice. Furthermore, she had none of that professional jealousy one encounters so often among singers. On the contrary, Katya was so full of admiration for the Spanish woman's mastery that she would forget everything else as she watched her during rehearsals, falling in love with her as surely as José! What a magnificent Carmen she was: fiery, sinuous, moving across the stage as lithely as a panther, her voice rich and passionate, truly a temptress who could make a soldier cast aside all considerations of allegiance and military honor. Caught up by the splendor of the lead singer's artistry, Katya found it hard to remain calm and concentrate. Moreover, Katya was singing Michaela's part, and the forgiving, long-suffering nature of this deceived young girl was one that Katya found alien. Yet despite this, Katya found favor with the audience, and the day after the young Russian singer made her debut, the press—while noting her youth and certain lack of assurance—was full of praise for her voice. Her voice was really very unusual: although it was powerful and could easily fill the auditorium, it did not have the metallic quality that is frequently a feature of strong voices. Without losing any power, it always remained smooth and round, its passage from note to note reminiscent of a violin, pure and precise.

The role of Tosca was much closer to Katya's heart: consuming love, jealousy, natural passion, self-sacrifice, all these emotions found an echo in those emotions which were stirring in Katya's own soul. She made an unforgettable Tosca, singing freely and fearlessly, oblivious to her surroundings.

Her performance was greeted with ovations and shouts of joy; she took curtain call after curtain call. The two first rows of seats in the stalls were thrust aside, some were broken. The applause and the admiring shouts of the fiery Italian audience blended into a mighty roar which left Katya stunned.

She stood there, drained, overjoyed, and grateful. She did not dare believe that she had managed to convey all her feelings to the people filling this enormous hall; she could not credit that her singing had brought forth this storm!

Exhausted yet full of joy, Katya and Grandmother returned to their hotel. Hard on their heels, the first bouquets began to arrive, and soon there was not a spare inch of space for the flow of tributes. Katya did not go to bed but sat out on the balcony until dawn. In any case, it would have been impossible—if not downright dangerous—to try to go to sleep inside because of the overwhelming perfume of the countless bouquets and baskets of blooms which filled every room. Grandmother, too, brought a chair out onto the balcony and sat in a corner behind Katya. Neither of them spoke. At times it seemed to Katya that Grandmother was either sighing heavily or crying, but she did not turn around because all the emotions of the evening seemed to have left her incapable of feeling anything. It seemed to her that her whole life, everything that had happened before this memorable evening, had gone forever, that it was the past and had disappeared beyond recapturing.

Milan slept around her in a rosy haze of dawn. And suddenly she felt as though a searing, bright flame had ignited in her heart, the pitiless flame which consumes everything in its path and fills the heart and soul to the exclusion of everything else in life, the flame which is love of Art.

Her bleak and needy childhood, her hard-working father and ever-strict mother, the magical meeting with the omnipotent maharajah-prince, his wealth, his gentle charm and kindness—

in her mind, all this was now no more than a small handful of cold cinders. All she wanted now was to carry the torch of this sacred flame, forsaking all else, to lose herself in music, deeper and deeper. To live only for her art, that was Katya's one desire, her reason for existence.

She sat there, turning over a host of recent memories in her mind. One of her teachers, Maestro Bimboni, was always very harsh and demanding in his studies with Katya, frequently reducing her to tears. His eyes burning with Latin fury, he would stamp his feet and shout, "Feeling! Feeling, I say! Do you hear me? Feeling!!!" followed by a string of Italian curses and imprecations. Once he raised his hands to the heavens and implored the Virgin Mary to ensure that Katya be seduced and then betrayed by someone, then rounded on his pupil and yelled, "Maybe *then* you'll finally learn what it means to love and to feel!" Seeing her tears, however, he relented slightly and groaned, "Those damned Russian snows have frozen your soul . . . Ridiculous, that's what it is! Such eyes, such a voice, *such* a voice, and your heart is nothing but a lump of ice!"

When Maestro Bimboni conducted the orchestra and, flinging back his mane of white, curly hair, raised his baton before the overture, time seemed to stand still. His ear was capable of detecting the slightest inaccuracy, the slightest hint of incorrect pitch in the orchestra, and woe betide the guilty musician who would be speared by the eye of the conductor!

Just before Katya's first performance of *Tosca*, Maestro Bimboni came to her dressing room and gathered her cold fingers into his large, warm hand.

"Today, little girl, sing freely, but keep your eye on my baton. The orchestra will be following your voice, let yourself be carried by the music. Forget about everything else. And don't worry—don't forget that I'm right there."

And Katya sang. It was as though she had plunged into an ocean of sounds and feelings. From time to time, her eyes would meet those of the conductor. They were stern yet kindly and gave her new strength before releasing her again. This support, invisible to all but Katya and her teacher, heartened and encouraged her to new heights. The orchestra was superb and melded beautifully with the singer's voice. She did not need to fear any dissonance or loss of rhythm. Her whole being seemed to become part of the music. And then, quite unexpectedly, she grasped that divine duality of an artist, without which true art cannot be attained. It was as though one Katya sang and expressed the most moving and powerful emotions, while another one stood by and watched, calmly and professionally, controlling and moving the alter ego on the stage. She could, with this new vision, see herself.

When the heavy folds of the curtain closed for the last time, Maestro Bimboni was the first to come running.

"*Mio angelo custodio!* (O, my guardian angel!)" he cried, kissing her in front of the whole troupe and falling to his knees in front of her. Tears poured down his cheeks. Katya bent down and put her arms around his head. "Stand up! I beg of you, please stand up!" she whispered. He got to his feet, and she put her arms around the old man, feeling his warm tears falling on her bare arms. Then she was approached by Maestro Guerci, who taught her drama. He removed his favorite signet ring from his finger—it was an ordinary, inexpensive ring, made of coral like all Italian rings, but the significance lay in the gesture. Katya was moved to tears. Placing the ring on her finger, he said, "Let my signet ring wed you to Art. Wear it always, so that it will remind you of what I taught you! Today is a great day not just for you, but for all of us, for it has seen the birth of a great singer and actress!"

The orchestra crowded around, somebody threw a shawl around Katya's shoulders, and someone put an arm around her and led her backstage. Grandmother—always so proud and domineering—burst into tears and kissed Katya's hand before Katya, bemused by everything, could pull it away.

The night wore on. Katya sat as though she were in an

enchanted dream. Russia seemed an incredibly distant childhood memory. Life, full of mystery and promise, lay before her, its roads leading all over the world, a world which seemed to lie at the feet of the young singer. The blue sky of eternally young Italy brightened above her, heralding the coming day and the morning of a new life.

Milan stirred and came awake. Newspapers carrying Katya's photograph and rave reviews were delivered. Maestro Bimboni arrived shortly afterward. He wore evening dress but, as an artist, permitted himself the license of wearing a large, white silk bow tie. Morning coffee and breakfast were a merry affair: the maestro even allowed Katya to drink a glass of wine. All the toasts he proclaimed were in her honor. Katya took out her red, leatherbound notebook, which contained a list of all the operatic roles she could perform, painstakingly written out in her neat, still rather unformed hand. Together with Maestro Bimboni, they bent their minds to deciding which ones she should take up next. Katya's breath seemed to catch in her throat. Was it really possible to "live" so many lives? To experience so many loves? To go through so many transformations? To sing of human happiness and suffering in such a way as to bring pleasure into people's lives, to open their hearts to compassion, kindness, purity?

Her own preference, her secret ambition, was to sing Margarita in *Faust.* But what had happened to Maestro Bimboni? Where was all his habitual strictness? He looked upon Katya now with love and admiration, smiling, his eyes half-closed as he hummed this or that snatch out of *Tosca.*

"Beautifully sung!" he would murmur, smiling happily. "Sung as if by an Italian . . ."

For Katya, this was the highest accolade possible. In the meantime, a crowd had gathered in the street outside the hotel, waving newspapers, pointing up to Katya's windows, taking off their hats in salute and inundating the hotel doorman with bouquets for the young singer. The chambermaid brought in an endless number of visiting cards, and now and then various enterprising persons would manage to gain entry on all sorts of pretexts: there were journalists asking for interviews, representatives of theaters from other cities, and of course many impresarios. Behind them, unseen, lurked businessmen of all kinds. All these people were drawn like bees to a pot of honey. That voice, that superb voice—even if it belonged to someone else, with a bit of enterprise it could make a lot of money for others, too.

Katya was offered a dazzling array of contracts, leading to all corners of the globe. This time Grandmother made no attempt to interfere, but left it up to Katya to make her own choice. Finally she signed a contract to do a full opera season in Buenos Aires: it was by far the most lucrative of all the offers she had received. She was given a bank draft for a sum far beyond her wildest dreams and held a handful of glittering gold coins in her hand.

That same evening, an urgent telegram arrived from Russia. It was signed by the prince and read, "Return immediately, your father dying. Have forwarded money to cover costs for cancelation of Buenos Aires contract."

The journey back to Russia was like a protracted nightmare. Both women traveled in tears and could not understand why they had been summoned to Moscow. Why was Grandfather, who lived in Kiev, dying in Moscow? And why was the prince himself not in Petersburg? Why was he in Moscow, too? They dreaded the possibility that Grandfather had already died and that they were being called back for his funeral.

Moscow at last—it was cold and damp; thick, wet snow fell onto gray, muddy streets, finding its way into clothing and sticking to faces and hands. They were met at the station by the prince, who was clearly in a state of considerable agitation.

"Forgive me," he said to both of them. "Forgive me . . . I

have acted very badly . . . I deceived you. But there was nothing else I could do. There was no other way to bring you back to Moscow! Prokofi Semyonovich is alive and well. I called you back because I love Katya and want to marry her. If she became an opera singer, even if she became world famous, that would have made our marriage impossible. I would never be able to call her my wife. I have asked Prokofi Semyonovich to come to Moscow for this reason, too. Now it is up to you to decide— my fate is in your hands . . ." He said all this without looking at them, his eyes on the wooden planks of the platform, but as he spoke the last words, he raised his head and looked straight into Katya's eyes.

Heedless of the people around them, heedless of the presence of her mother, Katya threw herself into his arms. She was weeping. From joy, or from sorrow?

12
"Unexpectedly and Forever"

*M*y parents' marriage produced a storm of speculation and rumor. The consensus of opinion was that an obscure young Polish nobody had managed to set herself up for life by snaring a besotted old man. But how could they understand that Katya had been faced with two choices, and how could the future of a young princess with an elderly husband—for all his wealth and palaces—stand comparison, even for a moment, with the worldwide recognition she could have had as a singer? It seems to me that Father, at the age of seventy-three, felt that he could do whatever he wished. Why should he bother about the displeasure of the tsar? How much longer did he have to live? What did he have to lose? What should he fear at the end of his life, not far from the grave? As for Mother— young, talented, beautiful, standing on the threshold of fame—she sacrificed all that forever.

I must confess that neither in my mind nor in my heart can I find understanding (I dare not say justification) for my father's action. I cannot help feeling that it was a cruel game to take into his hands a young, talented creature, to foster that talent and allow it to catch fire from the flame of Art, and then snuff out that fire on the threshold of fame and happiness. Nobody could condemn the prince for falling in love with Katya, but why did he not, as an undoubtedly kind and honorable man, refrain from taking advantage of her innocently unconcealed feelings for him? Why did he not, at his age, conquer his passion out of love for Katya? He took everything away from her and drew her into an abyss of which he was perfectly well aware. Enjoying a rank and position at court that made it possible for him to enter the presence of the tsar unannounced, he knew that he was therefore bound by certain responsibilities, that he had to observe certain rigorous norms, that there were bounds beyond which he could not go, and that he was not, ultimately, his own master. His rank and his position at court meant that he could not marry just to please himself: any marriage needed royal approval.

Yet now, alongside the ludicrous difference in ages, whom had he chosen as his bride? A girl from a family of long-impoverished Polish nobility, who had been born in some obscure Ukrainian backwater! He could not have been unaware of the dismay this would provoke in the coldhearted, hypocritical, disdainful, and intrigue-ridden circles of the court. He must have known that these circles would despise and smear his young wife. He could not have failed to foresee that.

All that I have written thus far about my mother's life was not drawn from recollections of witnesses or even from her own words. I have simply retold the contents of the diary she kept before her marriage. She burned this diary before her death during the war, in 1945. Before she did so, she said to me in her usual cold way, "I know that you have written since you were a child and that you're scribbling something now, too. I suspect that it's your dream to write 'memoirs,' which won't be of any use or interest to anyone. I also know that your cold and ungrateful mind will not spare anything or anyone. You're quite capable of publishing anything that you consider useful or interesting. Because of that, I don't want you reading my diaries after I'm dead."

And then and there, right in front of me, she tore the diaries up sheet by sheet and threw them into the burning stove. She burnt everything, every page of those diaries, which had been bound together into one leather-covered volume. Poor Mama! . . . I am so much at fault before her! I am at fault even now for doing what she wanted to prevent and admit my guilt. For I had read through all those diaries down to the last letter a long, long time before she destroyed them. I read through them in the long and terrible nights of 1919–20, sitting by her bed where she lay on the brink of death from typhus.

I hope that I will be believed when I say that I was not motivated by idle curiosity. I did not read those diaries as a daughter wanting to ferret out her mother's secrets. My heart almost seemed to stand still as I read, almost as though I were holding something sacred in my hands. I did not weep, but there were unseen, internal tears that washed away the black stone of doubt which had lain concealed in my heart for many years. I saw my mother in all the chastity and purity of her devotion and fidelity to her husband—her first and last love. No other male name appeared so much as once on any page of those diaries. Even the entries made in Italy—Palermo, Naples, Mentone—mention only him, memories of him. The desire to dedicate herself to Art and to belong to no man—all that was a result of what she believed to be her unrequited love for the prince. It should be noted that my mother was twenty-five years old when she married, and in those days it was customary for girls to marry before reaching twenty. Refusing all offers for her hand, she was clearly not worried by the prospect of remaining an "old maid."

I would not wish to join my voice to that mass which can accept only the most conventional understanding of what constitutes a marriage and decries anything that does not fall into the framework of the most basic definition just because it is different. Is it just, when learning of a marriage, to subtract the lesser age of one of the partners from the greater age of the other and, on the basis of this exercise in arithmetic, question the sincerity of their love? And in any case, can anything work greater miracles than a loving human heart? Can one set limits on the feats and sacrifices of which it is capable?

Grandfather was absolutely devastated. His friendship with the prince had grown and strengthened over the years. They held each other in esteem and respect, and then . . . what a bombshell! The prince's proposal to Katya was a terrible blow to Grandfather. He could not understand his friend, nor could he respect him any longer. Grandfather was a strict, just, and highly principled man, and he considered the prince's feelings and proposal unacceptable. He made no secret of this viewpoint. Having spent his life in poverty and unremitting toil, Grandfather was neither impressed nor tempted by the prince's wealth, considering it monstrous that his daughter should become the wife of an old man of seventy-three.

Seeing that he could not sway Katya from her resolve to marry the prince, Grandfather said to her, "Until now, I have spoken to you as a loving father appealing to his favorite daughter, but now I must address you as a doctor of many years experience. As a medical man, I cannot but forbid this unnatural marriage. The prince is forty-eight years older than you—that is an enormous gap! You must realize that he cannot live for much longer, and, when he dies, you will be left unhappy and alone. Have you thought of that? Luckily, there is no chance that you would have children, for they would be bound to be degenerate freaks, whom it would be a crime to bring forth into the world. Have you thought what it would be like for you to be left, a young widow, in the midst of an alien aristocratic society? And how you would cope with such a life, for which you are prepared to abandon the stage? I could almost believe that the old prince has hypnotized you. What other explanation can there be for your loss of willpower, for your readiness to give up the results of so many years of learning? You don't seem to care about your music any longer, you have thrown away your life's ambition! Katya, my dear child, what has come over you? All I can say is that, if I cannot talk you out of this ill-considered, irrevocable and monstrous mistake, it means that you do not trust and love me, your father, as much as you should!"

These words came as a great blow to Katya. Her father had always been an authority to her; he was her heart and her truth.

In the meantime Grandfather sought to reason with the prince. "What is it that you want to accomplish?" he demanded. "You know that you are not free to marry without the permission of the tsar! And who, in their right mind, would give their consent for a marriage when there is a forty-eight-year difference in the ages of the bride and groom? To say nothing of the fact that we are an impoverished family, which has long ago lost its lands and its right to the title of count? In fact, we are now nothing but ordinary gentry. Katya is a child, her grateful heart loves you for all that you have done for her, her feelings for you cannot be anything other than a reflection of that gratitude and the childish hero-worship she always had for you. But what about you? I hope you will not take it amiss when I remind you that you and I are almost the same age, and therefore I feel that I have the right to be frank with you. At your age of seventy-three, what you feel is not love, but a desire to possess a young creature. You have canceled out all the good you did her, and the payment you are demanding for your charity—her young life—is an aberration and a sacrilege!"

Grandfather's uncompromising denunciation and the sight of Katya's tears and grief over the breach with her father acted powerfully on the prince, and he retreated. He simply lost courage and told Grandfather that he was prepared to give up the girl he loved for the sake of her peace and happiness.

In her diary Katya noted that Grandfather said nothing to
her about his confrontation with the prince or about the prince's
decision. He merely told her that the prince wanted to see her
because he had something important to say to her. This meeting
duly took place at the beginning of November, on an afternoon
in the prince's house on Tverskaya Street.

Full of foreboding, Katya entered the prince's study. It was
twilight. The study was dimly lit by several candelabra on the
marble mantelpiece above the grate, in which a fire was burning.
As usual, the prince kissed Katya's forehead, and then went to
stand by the fireplace, his face in shadow.

"Katya," he began. "First of all, I admit that I am greatly at
fault—"

"You're going to tell me something terrible?" she interrupted fearfully.

"On the contrary," he replied with what seemed to be unruffled composure, "what I want to do is to avert 'something
terrible' . . . hear me out before you say anything more." And he
went on to tell her in detail how he had struggled against his
own feelings, how he had sent her to Italy in the hope that his
feelings would die down in her absence, even though her time
there was the fulfillment of the promise he had once given to
do all that lay in his power to help her become a brilliant singer.
He knew that the attainment of this ambition would make marriage between them impossible. Yet while she was away, he was
tormented by love and jealousy; he had traveled to Italy himself
to watch her secretly; he had even stooped to hiring professional
agents who, like hunting dogs, followed close on her heels wherever she went and submitted detailed reports about her life and
doings. He felt as though he were beginning to go mad . . . and
then came her operatic debut, news of the phenomenal success
she had enjoyed, about the contract which would have taken
her across the ocean to another part of the world entirely. And
then, casting aside all thought of honor, he had sunk to perpe-
trating an unforgiveable deception: he had sent a telegram full

of lies to two trusting women, forcing them to return to Russia. At the same time, he had summoned Katya's father to Moscow from Kiev. All this in the frantic hope that somehow he would be able to persuade her and not lose the woman on whom his entire happiness depended.

"It is not too late even now," he concluded. "You have full freedom of choice. It is only a few days since your first performance in *Tosca*. Here is sufficient money"—he pointed to a pile of checks on his desk—"for you to return to Italy tomorrow or the day after, resume your contract or sign a new one. I am an old man, a very old man, and I have no right to aspire to happiness with you. And there is the question whether you would be happy with me. Might you not come to regret it?"

"You're not sure?" asked Katya, her voice shaking. "You're going back on everything? You're casting me aside? Is it that you don't love me, or are you just afraid that court etiquette forbids you to marry me?"

"Yes . . . I don't want to comfort you with lies. Your father is right. Of course, I could follow my own inclination, but what kind of a life would it be? Just think, how much longer do I have to live? My days are numbered, and you would be left quite alone. Everything would fall on you. . . . Our marriage might not be recognized . . . Are you prepared for that?"

Katya was astounded by the calm way in which he spoke. Unable to see his face in the uncertain light, she could not believe her ears. She took a step forward, and the wavering candlelight illuminated his face for a moment, showing her how greatly he was suffering. He was ashen, and tears poured down his grief-stricken face.

A storm seemed to burst in her heart. The growth of their love flashed before her in a split second. The bracelet he had placed on her wrist: "Unexpectedly and forever." Had he not experienced a multitude of emotions? How much had each one of them suffered before they realized that they were bound together irrevocably? She remembered many other girls, her contemporaries, whose education had been sponsored by the prince: actresses, painters, ballerinas—had they been less attractive and talented? Had they not swarmed around him, seeking his favor, approval, and attention? And Katya's jealous heart had been unable to detect any sign of preference, any sign of anything other than simple kindness from him to them.

Katya and the prince had secretly loved each other for a long time. But finally he was prepared to do anything to gain his heart's desire. He brought them back from Italy under false pretenses and blurted out his proposal at the station like an awkward schoolboy, then had to submit to the indignity of listening meekly to the insulting strictures delivered by Katya's father, bearing it all uncomplainingly because he loved her. Was it not love for her that had precipitated him into this maelstrom of emotions, made him forget everything, expose his innermost feelings and, at his age, defend his love before the world, the love of his declining years? And now, tangled up in this web as if bereft of reason, he was again proposing to send her far away, this time forever. And he would remain alone in Russia, with an empty heart in an empty house, surrounded by portraits of his dead ancestors, alone, quite alone. His words "our marriage might not be recognized" echoed in Katya's ears. In an outburst of sacrifice, she laid her maidenly virtue and her heart at his feet. "I don't care about the marriage!" she cried, pressing herself to the breast of this man she loved above all else. "Nobody in the world matters apart from you! Don't talk to me about your age, don't say anything about dying! I want to be with you, to love you, never be parted from you! If you could find yourself in trouble because of me, if there is anything that might disturb your peace, then take my love just as it is. I don't need your name or your title. I don't care anything about the tsar's permission or the approval of the court. I don't even care if we cannot have the blessing of the Church!"

These words of love were like a healing ocean of balm on the suffering, doubt-torn heart of the prince. "I can never accept such a sacrifice, Katya, nor could I be happy if I were to do so. My happiness lies in being able to call you my wife!"

Her love overwhelmed and conquered him. This is how that meeting was described in Katya's diary. I discovered an echo of it on the reverse side of a photograph of my father, written in his own hand.

At this time, we were beset by trials, grief, doubts and painful partings. But all this seemed immaterial by comparison with the joys of love which we experienced in that immeasurable closeness, which made it possible to view even our sufferings as happy memories.

When we decided to join our lives forever, I found in my wife all that I had dreamed of, all that I could have wished for in my helpmate, if only . . . I thought of marriage, if I had not been certain that I have no right to fall in love, that I am too old for dreams, too late to hope for the impossible, that I had no right to bind the fate of this wonderful, scintillating young creature to mine! . . . But her faithful and loving heart overcame my fears and prejudices. I became her husband—the happiest of mortals. Prince Alexander Vasilyevich Meshchersky 10 November 1895.

The marriage took place on the night of November 10, 1895 at the regimental church of the Alexander Barracks across the Moskva River. They had chosen to marry in Moscow, at night, and in this obscure church, in order to ensure secrecy. The prince married without applying for permission to Tsar Nicholas II.

Here is an extract from a poem written by one of the people present, Professor Victor Ostrogradsky, which I found in Mother's trinket box after her death.

The buildings across the Moskva river are cloaked in darkness,
Carriages drive back and forth, seeking the holy church,

At last! The church and altar,
The aged gray-haired priest leads forth the bride and groom . . .
He stood there, tall and proud, this titled noble
This Russian prince, this faithful son of God.
And she—a beauty from the Ukraine, a genius, a dream . . .
Pronounce their vows at night, this happy pair . . .

After the ceremony, the newlyweds left for their palace near Poltava. Katya was radiantly happy; she remained the same Katya and gave no thought to the fact that she was now a princess. The difference in ages and the respect bordering on worship she felt for the prince all her life made it impossible for her, even as his wife, to address him by the familiar "thou." This seemed odd to many people, but she always addressed him with the formal "you" and as "Prince." I believe this formality was more for the benefit of the outside world than anything else, for it seemed to her strange to call him by any name other than his title in front of other people.

As I write, I have before me a small, old book, *Faith of the Heart,* written in French. This book was a present from the prince to the fiancée who was to become his first wife. Inside, inscribed in her hand in French, are the words, "Liza Stroganov. Given to me by Alexander. April 1848." Father was twenty-six years old at that time. Further, in his hand, are the words, "To my dear Liza from a friend." Forty-seven years later, when the prince married my mother, ornate bronze clips were attached to this yellow leatherbound volume. A photograph of Father is on the fly sheet under a thin sheet of glass, and under it are two names embossed in gold: "Sasha-Katya." In Mother's handwriting, there is an annotation: "Sashunya's favorite book, given to me in the days of our marvelous happiness. 1895."

So that was how she thought of him in her heart, hiding this pet name from all those curious eyes that watched their relations. And another note made by Mother: "Thank you, infinitely merciful God, for that great happiness, the bliss which you sent me, the most insignificant of all creatures, in making me the gift of such a kind, wonderful husband! Five years of joy."

But their happiness unleashed such a storm that it needed a man of Father's strength of character and pride to withstand it, to say nothing of a constitution which, in another man of his years, would have succumbed to a heart attack! Of course, news of the secret wedding leaked out, but Father had no enemies cruel enough to report him to the tsar. The first person to start persecuting the prince was his own daughter, Lily, Duchess Natalia Sasso–Ruffo, who, as I have said, lived in Italy and had three daughters of her own—Elsa, Maria, and Olga. Naturally, she had assumed that, when her father died, she would inherit all his wealth, which would in due course pass to her daughters. When she heard of Father's marriage, she sprang to the defence of her inheritance like a maddened she-wolf, fearing that her daughters—Father's granddaughters—would be deprived of their due. I have never blamed her for this, because nobody believed that my mother genuinely loved my father.

Lily sped to Russia and began to gather "information" about my mother. This gave rise to a stream of malicious gossip, speculation, and innuendo. Suddenly, any number of people emerged who remembered the suicide of Mama's fiancé Ivan Gardinsky; some of the Gardinskys' friends dug out the slanderous notices that had been posted throughout Kiev. Gossip depicted Gardinsky as a wronged, betrayed fiancé who could not bear the dishonor of his betrothed's becoming the prince's mistress. All this was set out in detail in a petition forwarded by the duchess to the tsar. She implored the tsar to take her "obviously senile" father into his custody, for clearly he had been entrapped into marriage by his young mistress, a Polish-Jewish cabaret singer. The duchess called upon Nicholas II to declare her father unfit to handle his own affairs and to freeze all his assets.

What infuriated the tsar above all was that the prince had married without royal consent, and, since he had done so, this must mean that everything written about him by no less a person than his own daughter must be true. In his wrath, the tsar stripped Father of all his honors, rank, and military decorations.

Father did not deign to respond to any of this. He did not feel any obligation to justify himself before the tsar. As for his daughter, he cursed her and cast her off forever.

At this point, intercession came from another quarter, from my grandfather. Since his fruitless attempt to block the marriage between his daughter and the prince, he had broken off all contact with the Meshcherskys. He did not give them his blessing, nor did he attend the wedding. When he heard about the duchess's actions and the substance of her petition to the tsar, however, he prepared himself for a trip to Petersburg. He gathered all the documents concerning the Podborskys, birth certificates, maps of their former land holdings in Poland. He also obtained a history of the family and a copy of the family crest. Then he gathered all the papers concerning Katya: her secondary school and Moscow Philharmonic graduation certificates, copies of programs from her concerts, the posters advertising her opera debut in Milan, and a thick file of reviews. Grandmother pulled his old general's uniform out of a large, ironbound trunk for the occasion, a uniform he wore for the last time on this trip to Petersburg.

Upon his arrival in Petersburg, Grandfather submitted a request for a royal audience. Even though the tsar had been angered by the whole affair, he was clearly also quite curious about it for Grandfather was granted an audience very quickly and with no difficulties.

Grandfather was a man of few words and left no written memoirs, so I am unable to say what transpired during this meeting. Only the outcome is known. An overjoyed Grandfather turned up at Vesely Podol, bearing a personal letter for the prince from the tsar. Nicholas invited Father to come to court, adding that he would personally see to it that the duchess would be punished for slandering her father. The tsar also adjured the prince to bring his young wife to court, for her position meant that she should be included in the ranks of the tsarina's ladies-in-waiting. What had occurred, wrote the tsar, was a regrettable misunderstanding which had now been cleared up. The letter was addressed to Father by rank, which meant the restoration of all his orders and honors.

One might have supposed that the quarrel between two such old friends as Father and Grandfather would have been patched up on this occasion, but it was not to be. The prince was very angry with Grandfather and, to everyone's dismay, immediately sat down and wrote a defiant reply to the royal summons. A notarized copy of this letter was confiscated from us in 1930. By chance, Mother retained a much-amended hand-written draft of this missive. It reads:

> I thank your Imperial Highness for the honor offered. I am an old man; I have turned 73. Like all Meshcherskys, I wore a military uniform and defended my native land. You are the fourth tsar of my country whom I have served. As a mark of recognition of my long and faithful service, I would ask that you release me from any return to the court, and let me live out what is left of my life on my estate in Poltava. As for the duchess, it is not for you, Your Highness, to judge her, but God shall judge between father and daughter after our deaths. I have laid a curse on her, as is my parental right. When I die, it is my will that she be kept away from my funeral.

There was no reply to this letter, but it was reported back to Father that the tsar was very displeased with him.

Father's anger with Grandfather remained unabated. "Why did you go to bend the knee to the tsar?" he demanded.

But Grandfather had his pride, too. "Rest assured that it was not to seek the restoration of Prince Meshchersky's honors," he retorted. "I went to try to cleanse my innocent daughter of some of the dirt that has come her way with your princely crown. I didn't talk about the Meshcherskys to the tsar, but about the Podborskys!"

The rift between my father and grandfather deepened. Grandfather was a very proud man. In the eight years of my parents' marriage, he never accepted a single present or any financial assistance from them, nor did he come to stay as a visitor at the palace, even though the rest of the Podborskys clung to Mother like leeches. Grandfather continued his unremitting toil, and his daughter's brilliant marriage made no difference whatsoever to his lifestyle.

In 1898 my mother bore a son, my older brother, Vyacheslav. This did bring Grandfather hotfoot, his concern sharpened by the fact that he was a medical man. He examined the baby thoroughly and was fully satisfied that all was well. That evening he even drank a glass of champagne with the prince and congratulated him on the birth of his heir. The birth of a grandson mellowed Grandfather considerably, but he remained true to himself, and all the visits he paid were very fleeting ones.

My brother's godfather was the Grand Duke Mikhail Alexandrovich Romanov, the tsar's brother. He tried time and again to persuade Father to return to the court, but with no success. Father remained adamant.

My brother was a true child of love and inherited the best features of both parents: Father's height and build; and Mother's beauty, the same chestnut hair, the same gentle, velvety brown eyes, which could nonetheless sparkle with mischief and mirth. Even before he learned to speak, he showed an iron will and demanded everyone's submission. Mama was very surprised once when she went up to his crib and saw that he was fast asleep, firmly clutching a large military hip flask. In answer to Mama's query, Vyacheslav's nursemaid said that he had cried until the flask was taken down off the wall, where it hung along with a number of weapons, and given to him. He was unable to say what he wanted, but kept pointing. From that day on, to the nurse's dismay and total conviction that "the little prince would be an alcoholic," Vyacheslav refused to go to sleep without that flask. Father and Grandfather, on the other hand, thought it was a great joke. Later, when my brother learned to talk, it turned out that he was extremely possessive. He adored his nurse and was jealous of anything that distracted her attention from him. "You can look only at me," he would state. "You can love only me and talk to me!"

Like most children from aristocratic families, we were denied the joy of being breast-fed by our mother. I do not know whose idea it was, but the wet nurse hired for Vyacheslav was most unusual. She was a very beautiful gypsy. She was supervised by two nursemaids (who played the role of warders), and it was their job to keep an eye on her, because she was madly in love with our handsome blacksmith and had a tendency to climb out of the nursery window straight into the park to keep assignations with him. The nursemaids would follow her, shouting reproaches, and hustle her back to the nursery. I am sure that with her milk my brother absorbed the fiery, boundless *joie de vivre* which was noted by all. Daring and fearlessness were key features of his character.

Life in the Poltava palace was full of events and excitement: visits from the neighboring gentry, balls, amateur theatricals, horse-racing on thoroughbred steeds—all this ebullient, hectic existence went to Mother's head like a drug. I suspect that my father arranged matters like that deliberately. Is it not strange that he did not want any further extension of her education, a closer acquaintance with literature, a maturing of her spiritual interests and values? Is it not strange that anything which might have contributed to her inner growth and development was painstakingly avoided? Under his influence, pliable as wax, Mama's mental and spiritual self fell asleep. She hardly ever went near the piano. Occasionally, she would sing a little to entertain visitors—light Italian canzonettas, folk songs, or French romances—but that was all. She was like a bird in a gilded cage.

Grandmother, however, positively bloomed. She could still not accustom herself to the idea that her son-in-law was a prince and her daughter a princess. She seemed to grow younger, more attractive, as if undergoing a kind of second youth. From time to time, she would arrive to visit, always a noisy affair. Her prickly Polish pride made her imagine that the reception accorded her in the prince's home was not everything it should be. She was always imagining slights and seeing offense where none was intended; she constantly faced Mother with more and more demands. On one occasion, when one of the menservants addressed her as "Madam" instead of "Your Excellency" (he had no idea that she was a general's wife), Grandmother demanded that Mother dismiss that servant forthwith. Of course, Mama refused to do anything of the kind, so Grandmother enacted a hysterical scene and refused to come downstairs for dinner. Every time something like this happened, the prince would order the carriage brought around to take Grandmother to the station. She would leave in a huff, throwing annihilating glances at Mama as she marched out the door. Yet a week or so later she would be back, just as though nothing had happened.

My mother's two brothers, Nikolai and Dmitri (both officers), inundated Mama with letters enclosing the IOU slips of their gaming debts. There were also visits by the Bodnevskys. Olga's shameful elopement had been forgiven and forgotten, and she was on excellent terms with Grandmother and Grandfather.

Olga's husband spent his days shooting. As hunting was forbidden on all of our three estates, "Uncle Lyelyechka," as he wanted us to call him, tested his marksmanship, or perhaps showed off his marksmanship, by shooting at flowers and starlings, frightening everyone, as he was apt to open fire at any time of the day or evening.

Olga passed the time by writing skits, witty epigrams, and was the moving force in organizing amateur theatrical performances, picnics, and similar pleasures. Drawing on the resources of her now-rich sister, Olga published a book of her poems, dedicating it to her "beloved and incomparable sister," Princess Meshcherskaya.

The prince was also a prolific writer of poetry in an amateur sort of way, and this gave him something in common with Olga. Mama used to recall with a smile how Olga flirted madly with the prince, but when she realized that this would not produce the desired result, she wrote a poem entitled "The Mistake."

Amid the darkness, like a flash of light, I saw a living flame;
In the turbulent heart of a poet, a heart so near and clear to mine.
So did I think: the sound of lyres resounded in my trembling heart . . .
And blue forget-me-nots bloomed in my soul like gentle dreams.
Amid the darkness, like a flash of light, I saw a living flame . . .
But it was just a rocket's passage, so brilliant, yet so void!

Having reluctantly abandoned hope of seeing Katya become a world-famous singer, Grandmother once again favored Olga above her other children and would frequently look at her, shake her head, and whisper, *"This* is the one who should have become a princess!"

Anatolia spent most of her time wandering around the park and sketching. In view of Mama's musical talent, attempts had been made to teach Anatolia singing, too. As I have said, she had a very powerful voice, but was tone deaf. Her loud, false renditions of gypsy songs rang out in the park and throughout the palace. She had an annoying habit of closeting herself in the library and then leaving books and journals scattered in untidy piles all over the floor. When Mama asked her to be a bit more tidy, she would retort, "I'm not some petit bourgeois! I'm of gentle birth! What tedious small-mindedness to demand that each thing be put back in the same place!" Every time she spotted a good-looking footman, gardener, or coachman, she would half-close her eyes and exclaim, loudly and sincerely, "Oh, what a shame! *So* handsome, but a commoner!"

The servants of the house were in a state of considerable unrest. They remembered the prince's first wife and they recalled what they considered the former "proper tone" of life in the palace. The first princess had been no beauty, but she was a kind, quiet, and gentle creature. She had passed her days doing needlework, playing Chopin on the piano, and reading her small French prayer book. Occasionally, as a special treat, she would drive out in a carriage with her English companion, enjoy a game of croquet, or read sentimental French novels. Then Lily was born, and the servants watched her grow up, become a young lady, and then marry. The servants had warm memories of the late princess and had a deep respect for the many years that the prince had remained a widower. His marriage to my mother came like a bolt from the blue to the entire household. The prince is marrying again, and who is his bride? Even before they laid eyes on her, the servant's hall took a deep dislike to Mama. And even when they did see her and got to know her, the prejudices against her became even more entrenched. To them she was a "showgirl," an "usurper," and "not a real princess." The flame of their hatred was further fanned by the fact that Mama became the reason for the breach between prince and his daughter by his first marriage.

Every time Mama spoke to one of the female servants, she would invariably find herself facing some former nurse, maid, or attendant of her predecessor, and when she looked at the still, shaven faces of the male servants, she would see irony and even a trace of unspoken disrespect in their eyes. This, perhaps, was to be expected. The noisy, impulsive Podborskys seemed to be everywhere, and they seemed to turn everything upside-down. They all had a full measure of Polish temperament: they quarreled loudly and then made up just as loudly; shrieks of anger were interspersed with shrieks of pleasure and outbursts of raucous laughter.

Knowing the prince's habitual calmness, his good breeding, the servants watched and waited for the inevitable moment when the "spell" under which he was laboring would be broken, when "the scales would drop from his eyes" and the "Polish rule" would come to an end. Then the former orderly and "decent" way of life would be resumed. But then something happened that changed everything.

The power of childhood memories is known to everyone. The Podborsky sisters had vivid recollections of the little house in which they had lived, its overgrown garden and the local fruit and vegetable markets (known as *bashtans*). These piles of watermelons, canteloups, pears, and plums would be laid out on the ground near the tents of their vendors, surrounded by huge buckets of cherries, nuts, and wagonloads of dried fruits drawn by big, docile oxen chewing their cuds and surveying the world from large, melancholy eyes.

It was only occasionally that wafer-thin slices of canteloupe were served for dessert at the palace. Watermelon would be served, carved into elaborate shapes and filled with glacé fruits, so that it did not taste or smell anything like a real watermelon should. One day, Mama had an idea. She sent two of the serving girls to the market with a horse and ordered them to bring back an array of fruit. Everything they brought back was immediately concealed. After lunch, when everyone had withdrawn to their rooms to rest from the heat of the day, those privy to Mama's scheme sneaked off to a remote room on the second floor of the palace. They spread a carpet on the floor, and set out all the fruit on trays. The silk blinds were carefully drawn, and the conspirators sat down in the golden half-light to a real feast. They cut off large chunks of watermelon and canteloupe, cracked nuts, and devoured dried fruits and juicy Ukrainian pears.

The participants were Mama, both her sisters, a young Frenchwoman who had been hired for conversation practice, the resident pianist (it was her task to play at dances when no orchestra was present), and the two young maids who had acted as Mama's emissaries.

One of the older servants may have whispered a word to the prince about the "improper behavior" of the young princess, or perhaps he himself happened to notice the drawn blinds in the opposite wing of the palace and decided to investigate. But whatever the reason, the door of the room opened without warning at the very height of the "fruit feast," and the tall, thin, stern figure of the prince stood on the threshold.

For the first time in three years of marriage, Mama burst into tears. That day, dinner was served after a considerable delay. Father had led his weeping wife to her boudoir and closed the door behind them.

The old servants (the first princess's "champions") did not conceal their glee. At last! At last the prince would realize what a commoner he had married and what low tastes she had! The servants huddled in whispering groups, tried to listen at keyholes, and lurked in the corridors in the hope of catching a glimpse of something interesting. The person most affected by what had happened was Grandmother. First she wept, then she pretended to have a heart attack, then finally declared that she had a migraine and retreated to her bedroom with a damp towel wrapped around her head. There she sat, pouring out a despairing monologue: "It's terrible! Terrible! My daughters sitting there on the floor, stuffing themselves like savages! My God, everything is ruined! The shame of it! Sitting there cracking nuts and spitting out the shells just like the grooms in the stables! And the prince saw it all! Oh, it's awful, awful!" Olga and Anatolia huddled in a corner, sniffling. The Frenchwoman and the pianist waited to be paid off and dismissed. Olga's husband ordered their bags packed and sat glumly drinking cognac. The sharp odor of smelling salts permeated all the corridors of the palace.

Meanwhile, in the boudoir, Father was doing his best to comfort Mama. He spoke to her gently, laughed about the whole incident with complete sincerity, and assured her that he found the escapade delightful. Mama refused to be comforted, however, being convinced that he did not mean what he was saying, but really despised her for what she had done.

The upshot was that the prince issued an order legitimizing such fruit feasts, which were henceforth to be repeated in that same room and on the carpet. He even took part in them himself and had dessert wines brought up from his cellars, as well as sparkling mead aged there in sealed barrels. He further had the idea of having everyone attend the fruit feasts dressed in Ukrainian national costume, with beads, ribbons, garlands of flowers, the women plaiting their hair into long braids down their backs. Mama would join a chorus of young girls in singing the favorite Ukrainian songs of her youth: " 'Tis Eventide," "Farewell Kiev," "Oh, Do Not Go Out, Gritse," "What Need Have I of These Dark Eyes?" and many others. . . .

After this turn of events, the old guard of the first princess's servants had no choice but to adopt a low profile. They could see for themselves how the prince sat on the floor, on the carpet, holding a large slice of watermelon and eating it without a fruit knife or fork—worse still, he did not even use a plate. In their eyes, this was a dreadful, incomprehensible sight, for he, after all, was a "real" prince! The servants began to look more favorably on the young princess and, seeing her kindness and lack of pretension, gradually started to accept her. Some held out, so it can be said that the servants were divided into two camps, which, however, observed a peace of sorts.

Despite the total estrangement between the prince and his daughter, who had returned to her palazzo in Italy, Mama could not help feeling that she was surrounded by spies and that everything she did, as well as everything that happened in the

A side view of the entrance, Vesely Podol.

*T*wo guardians of the gate carved from Venetian stone.

Interior view of the Palace.

We managed to photograph the Palace several hours before it was blown up so the stone could be used for construction materials.

My husband and I with our boxer, Madzhi, standing at the former entrance of the Palace.

My husband and I standing where the family archives and the museum had been located.

The Palace ruins proved convenient for storing lumber.

My husband, Igor Sergeevich Bogdanovich, a person whose fate, like all those of our class, was a tragic one. He died in my arms on August 29, 1977, of a heart attack. His great-grandfather, Ippolit Fyodorovich Bogdanovich (1744–1803) wrote the celebrated narrative poem "Dushenka: An Ancient Tale in Free Verse," a Russian version of the myth of Amor and Psyche.

Conversing with a visitor in my apartment, January 1989.
PHOTOGRAPHER: VADIM KROKHIN

Faith and prayer sustained me through many ordeals.

PHOTOGRAPHER VADIM KROHKIN

palace, was known to the duchess down to the smallest detail, for long letters from various persons were sent off regularly to Italy.

After the opulent and ceremonial christening of my brother, his godfather, our father's close friend, Grand Duke Mikhail Alexandrovich, became an even more frequent visitor at Vesely Podol. With growing insistence, he pressed Father to return to court, as the tsar was waiting for Mama to be presented. All our Poltava neighbors added their urgings: the Kochubey princes, the Gudima-Levkoviches, the Rodziankos, and the charming Countess Miloradovna, who was later to be my godmother. She was a wonderful woman, talented and gifted with great intelligence. She wrote delightful poems and children's stories and was kind, cheerful, honest, and sincere. I do not know who finally broke the wall of Father's resistance and persuaded him to present Mama to the entire Russian royal family. According to Grandmother, the main force was not so much Countess Miloradovna, but her elderly mother, Princess Vasilshchikova, one of the favorite ladies-in-waiting of Dowager Empress Maria Fyodorovna.

I do know that, once they went to Petersburg, my parents stayed there for a considerable time. During their stay, a huge costume ball was held at the court. Mama went dressed as Queen Elizabeth of England, and still I have photographs of her in this costume. In one picture she is signing Mary Stuart's death warrant, and in the other she is standing upright, having signed the execution order, holding a quill pen in her hand.

I remember Mother describing how once, at a small, select reception at the royal palace, Countess Miloradovna appealed to her to sing. This request was upheld by everyone present. Mama tried to refuse, not knowing what Father's reaction would be. Then, suddenly—Mama was always visibly moved when she described this—Countess Miloradovna, clad in a diaphanous, snow-white silk gown and covered in diamonds, fell to her knees before Mama in front of the whole court and pleaded, "Little nightingale, little princess, I beg you, sing! I shall not get up until you do!"

Thrown completely off balance by the passionate plea of the expansive, original Countess Miloradovna, Mama could not refuse and started to sing. Everyone was enchanted, including the royal couple. Mama was asked to sing again and again, so she did. . . .

When Mother and Father returned home, Mama wept disconsolately for a long time. Looking at the handful of courtiers and listening to their French compliments, she recalled earlier ovations, that storm of delighted cries of "Bravo! Bravo! Bravissimo!" Italy, Milan, the adulation of the crowd. Possibly this concert awoke in her memories of unalloyed happiness, when it seemed that all she had to do was reach out and grasp the laurels of glory. She probably remembered how she had stood on the stage of the immortal Milan Opera, which opened roads to the rest of the world. She may also have recalled that cold morning at the station in Moscow, the first wet snow, and the pale, worried, rather desperate face of the prince, his unexpected proposal right there on the platform, the sight of his familiar carriage with the Meshchersky crest on the doors standing behind his thin, tall figure, a carriage drawn by swift, midnight-black horses whirling her further and further away from true happiness.

It seems to me that only such recollections could account for the tears she shed then—and never explained—and the wave of despair that suddenly washed over her.

She did not know that, after she had left Italy, Maestro Guerci sent her a long letter. This letter gave a detailed description of what happened at the first performance of *Tosca* following her departure for Moscow when another singer took over her role. True to his fiery Italian temperament, Maestro Bimboni broke his baton in half in the middle of the first scene, burst into tears, and left the hall. From that day on, he always refused to conduct another performance of *Tosca*. But Mama never saw that letter: it was intercepted by the prince.

Seeing the effect on Mama of this chance performance at court, the prince took her back to the Poltava estate immediately. He prevailed upon Mama to make two solemn vows: first, that she would never return to the court after his death and, second, that she would forget the stage forever and never perform again. Mother made these vows and kept both of them.

At that time, Prince Paolo Trubetskoy returned to Russia from abroad. He was just beginning to gain recognition as a sculptor, and it was thought that a brilliant future awaited him. Paolo (Pavel) had been raised in Italy. His father was already an elderly man when he married a young Italian who persuaded him to leave Russia and take her back to her native land. Prince Trubetskoy eventually died in Italy, leaving his young widow and their small son. The widow never returned to Russia, and Paolo's upbringing was entirely Italian. He spoke Russian very badly and with a strong foreign accent. His style of art belonged to the Expressionist school. Following his artistic perceptions, he would depict people symbolically.

It is hard to say what shaped Paolo's perception of the writer Leo Tolstoy, but he certainly did not depict him as a dry, thin old man, a thinker torn by inner conflicts and contradictions who with the wise yet implacable gaze of a fanatical sectarian moralized and passed judgment on everyone. Instead, in Paolo's representation, we see an elderly, rather portly man on horseback with the smug and well-fed expression of a self-satisfied merchant or a forester employed by a well-to-do master. . . . When Trubetskoy set about depicting the peaceful reign of Tsar Alexander III, which was unmarred by any internal upheavals or foreign wars, he made Alexander look like a fat, shapeless figure of fun perched on a huge horse with such a disgustingly exaggerated crupper that this sculpture became popularly known as "The Bogeyman." Our father, a thin old man with a kind and intelligent face, Paolo depicted as an immensely elongated, skeletal figure reminiscent of Don Quixote. This figure was dressed in military uniform, with a bony, gooselike neck surmounted by a thrown-back head and a face twisted into a fastidiously contemptuous grimace, something completely alien to Father as he really was.

Actually, Father took no offense. He had known Paolo since the latter was a baby, had been friendly with his father, and, whenever Paolo visited Russia, it was customary for him to stay at Vesely Podol for long periods. When he met Mama, Paolo immediately began to sculpt numerous figures of her, fell madly in love with her, and made her a marble figure of her favorite dog, "Pussy" (this sculpture was later nationalized). In fact, Trubetskoy lost his head so completely that he was unable to conceal his feelings from Father.

One of Paolo's best clay sculptures was of Mother on horseback, a sculpture he was to repeat later in bronze. Mama posed for him on horseback in the stables, at quite a distance from the artist, but every time he went up to her to adjust a fold of her riding dress or change some other detail, he would leap back as quickly as possible in a state of visible agitation as though he had been scalded. Then, returning to his clay, he would continue to work, whispering, "O, Holy Maiden!"

Trubetskoy had a swarthy complexion and was charming rather than handsome, with large, black, burning eyes. It cost Mother considerable patience to last through all the sittings needed.

"He has no manners whatsoever!" she complained to Father. "Either that, or he's completely mad!"

"No, he's simply in love with you," Father replied, "and that's not to be wondered at!"

He watched Paolo's growing passion and did nothing but laugh good-naturedly about it. But one evening, when he and Mother were alone, he suddenly turned to her and said quite seriously, "Katya, I can see that Paolo is very much in love with you, much more deeply than I thought at first. I don't want to upset you, but you are intelligent enough to look facts in the face. I can't have long to live now: my health is not what it used to be, nor is my strength. When I die, you should marry him. He will take you back to your beloved Italy."

Mama made no reply. The next morning, when the three of them sat down to breakfast, Mama turned to Trubetskoy and gently but courteously asked him to leave the house.

"This is my personal request," she told him, "and I would ask you to act upon it without asking questions or seeking explanations. But I ask you to do as I say. You have done nothing wrong; you have offended nobody; and I hope that you will believe me that I have no desire whatsoever to hurt you. But it would be best if you left."

Trubetskoy was very upset and could not understand what was wrong, but he had no choice. When he departed, Mama declined to keep a single sculpture of his as a memento, even though Father tried to persuade her to change her mind. She wanted no reminders of Paolo whatsoever.

Why had Father raised this matter at all with Mama? I find it hard to reconcile the fact that he, who had made Mama swear that after his death she would not return to society and would forgo the stage, nonetheless advised Mama to marry Trubetskoy when she became a widow! I can only explain the inconsistency of his behavior by a desire to test the strength of his wife's love for him and the degree of power he had over her. Yet it must be admitted that if he overstepped the bounds of what is acceptable in his last and consuming love, he was nevertheless a man of great sincerity, kindness, and honor. I shall limit myself to two examples, drawn from Mama's diaries, to illustrate the real nature of the man.

It was customary, when there was a change in village schoolteachers (and there were plenty of villages, because our Poltava estate consisted of no less than one and a half thousand hectares), the newly appointed teacher would report to the local landowner. I do not wish to name names, but one of Father's nephews could never be bothered about receiving the teacher and would send along a servant to give her fifteen rubles, "so that she wouldn't bother him about anything."

Once, when a large group of guests was being entertained at the Poltava palace and everyone was about to sit down to lunch, a peasant's gig drew up outside and an elderly woman alighted from it—a new teacher who had come to replace one who had recently died. She was a typical elderly provincial schoolteacher, wearing large steel-rimmed spectacles, with her hair pulled back into a bun, from which numerous hairpins protruded in all directions.

The footman who opened the door to her decided not to announce her arrival until after lunch. But Father had happened to glance out of the window as she was getting out of the gig, and asked the servants who she was. When he was told that it was the new village schoolteacher, Father, to everyone's amazement, ordered lunch to be delayed. He commanded that she be given a chance to wash and tidy up, and only after she had been shown into the dining room (somewhat discomfited by finding herself in such a large and noisy gathering!) did Father give the signal for lunch to be served. The poor woman did not feel at all comfortable among the assembled aristocracy and surrounded on all sides by conversations in foreign tongues. Foreseeing that this would be the case, Father had placed her beside him and devoted special attention to her during the meal.

When everyone adjourned to the salon for dessert and Turkish coffee, Father made his excuses to his guests and took the teacher off to his study. He listened attentively to all her requests and promised to help with everything, especially with establishing a library in her village. As this took place during the summer holidays, he invited her to stay for a while at Vesely Podol, but she declined on the pretext that she had to get back. She may simply have felt too ill at ease to accept this invitation. All the guests were surprised to see Father escorting the school-teacher through the palace back to the entrance hall. He then went out on the balcony and remained there until the gig, with its passenger, had moved away down the drive and was lost from view. Mama was rather surprised that Father had shown such extraordinary attention to a perfect stranger who had thus far done nothing to earn it. When she mentioned this to Father, he answered, "She must know that under my roof, all guests are of equal importance."

"But she came on business," expostulated Mama, "not as a visitor!"

"Yes, Katya, so she did. She did not come as a visitor, but as a supplicant. And having to ask for something is never easy. So it was up to me to do everything I could to make her task easier."

Another occasion, which when recounted later made many people laugh, was in fact a tragicomedy.

I do not think that all the conventions of our society in those days merit approval. For instance, I do not approve of the habit of kissing married women's hands or of the false "social" kisses people lavished on each other even if they were enemies. There was much that was silly and even downright unhygienic in everyday practice. For some reason, it was customary after dinner for servants to bring around large trays with "rinsers." These were tall, dark-blue crystal glasses, filled with a white, mint-flavored mouthwash and sitting in very deep opaque saucers. One would rinse one's mouth and spit the mouthwash out into these cuplike saucers. Even though the dark glass of the saucers obscured what you spat out, it was still rather unappe-

tizing to see guests who had just finished a delicious meal fall
silent and sit there earnestly rinsing their mouths in front of
each other, and then spitting out the result.

The incident recorded by Mama in her diary concerned
the unexpected arrival of a priest (rather like the unexpected
arrival of the schoolteacher) who had been sent by the Synod
to replace a priest who had died. Again like the schoolteacher,
he came to pay his respects to the prince. As usual, there were
a lot of guests at Vesely Podol and a large company had gathered
for dinner. The new priest was not young, but he radiated a
kind of innocent good nature. He was clearly impressed by what
he saw: the rooms, the palace itself, his host, and the people
among whom he found himself.

The priest turned out to be quite loquacious. During dinner, he seemed perfectly at ease, without trying to put himself
forward unduly, and drank very moderately. However, he had
obviously not had enough to quench his thirst after such a filling
meal and, when the servants brought around the mint-flavored
mouthwash, he obviously decided this was some new and original drink of which he had never heard. He drank the mouthwash in one gulp and asked the servant for more. Around the
table there was total silence; everyone was trying not to smile;
many had trouble stopping themselves from laughing. . . . The
prince looked slowly and coldly around the room, raised his
own glass of mouthwash to his lips, and slowly drank the whole
glass. Someone coughed nervously; someone else made a choking sound. Several took a sip or two from their own glasses;
others pretended to drink; some moved their glasses aside and
left them untouched. But nobody dared to use the mouthwash
for its real purpose.

After this, Father ordered that the glasses of mouthwash be
set out in the room adjoining the dining room. This was a long
service chamber through which food was brought to the dining
room from the kitchen. This change was greeted with enthusi-

asm, especially by the younger people, who abandoned the practice of rinsing after meals completely. Father could never, under any circumstances, tolerate people being mocked.

After the birth of my brother, Father decided to sell his house on Tverskaya Street in Moscow. Mama had no objections because she had unhappy memories of that house. It was here that she met and later had to confront her stepdaughter the duchess. As for Father, his motives were, as usual, jealousy. He did not want Mama to live in the city after he died and even made a virtue out of his selfishness by saying that it would be to Mama's ultimate benefit! The nature and the climate of the Ukraine, he asserted, would be much more beneficial for her and for their growing son. If she wanted a change of scene, there were always the other two estates for her to go to. Why bother with Moscow?

Vyacheslav was developing into a lively and very good-natured boy. Mama adored him as her firstborn, but Father was not quite as besotted. After he had cursed and cast off his daughter from his first marriage, he secretly hoped for another daughter to replace her. So when a son was born, he could not conceal his disappointment even in front of Mama. He had wanted a daughter. As for the Podborskys, they were fully aware that the prince was living out his last years, if not months. Therefore, they did everything they could to ingratiate themselves with the boy. In their eyes, he would inherit all his father's wealth, and they saw him as a future source of all kinds of bounty.

In 1902, a year before his death, Father continued his hobby of breaking in wild houses and training them to accept saddle and bridle. In early spring, despite the fact that he had a heavy cold, he set off on horseback with a group of friends to watch the ice breaking up on the river. He had been twice shot through the lungs in military actions, and, as a result of this expedition, he came down with pneumonia. The infection flared up like a kerosene-soaked wick touched by a match. Even though he recovered from this bout of pneumonia, it was the beginning of the end. His health was not fully restored, and his strength waned noticeably. Then his heart began to grow weaker. Mama was distraught, knowing that he could not last much longer. She became even more convinced of this when she found a sheet of paper, covered with his by-now-wavering writing, tucked into his Bible. It was a touching prayer which he had composed and written out but kept hidden from Mama. I am making it public to show the depth of his boundless, faithful, and honorable love for my mother.

O, Lord, who art Love! To Thee I am indebted for the sweetness of love and companionship; filling my heart with them, Thou hast granted me the greatest joys of mankind. O, Creator of the joy of mortals! Extend Thy blessing and bring salvation to the one who is the love of my heart: preserve her from the perils of life in this world and spread Thy protection over her, that evil shall not touch her. Be with her in all the paths of her life, and if sorrow should threaten her or foes seek to persecute her, be her Protector. O Lord of Grace, do not suffer her brow to be furrowed with suffering and cares. Grant her, O Lord of Mercy, all earthly needs: shield her soul from the tempest of grief, and if she should err through weakness, lead her back to virtue in humility. Do not punish her in Thy strict judgment, but extend to her the mercy of Thy boundless grace. I call upon the Guardian Angel bestowed by Thee to protect her in all her undertakings: that he should be by her always as a Guardian who shall finally bring our two souls together beyond the grave to the joy of pure and holy companionship without fear of parting.

I still have this prayer, written by my father on a thin, bluish piece of paper. I keep it in Mother's old, dark red wallet, which is embroidered with forget-me-nots. Later, Mama rewrote the prayer on a large sheet of thick paper and surrounded it with watercolor sketches of flowers and a cherub's head. I keep it in the same wallet.

Clearly, knowing that his end was near, Father realized how young and beautiful the wife was that he would leave behind. It seems obvious that he considered Mama's infatuations, errors arising from passion, and perhaps even long-term liaisons to be perfectly natural and only asked God for one thing, that He should not judge her too harshly, not punish her, but show her mercy.

"The foes who seek to persecute her," to whom he refers in the prayer, are without doubt that part of the aristocracy, headed by the duchess (how right his premonition was!), which could start a campaign against Mother after his death. And that is just what they did.

One cannot help smiling at the touching words at the end of the prayer in which he asks for the reunion of his soul with Mother's, with no mention of "dear Liza," his first wife.

Outwardly, life in the Poltava palace continued as usual: numerous guests, receptions, soirées. Father tried to appear hale and hearty, but the shadow of death could be seen in his tired face. Feeling impending doom and considering herself the cause of the estrangement between father and daughter, Mama felt terribly guilty and wanted nothing more than to bring about a reconciliation between the prince and the duchess. But every time she tried to bring up the subject with Father, it would result in an outburst of anger and a refusal.

Father, on the other hand, was worried by completely different considerations. Knowing that death was near, he felt it was vital to ensure that all the necessary legal steps be taken to ensure the correct disposal of his property after his death. However, he did not want to frighten Mama by openly making a will.

Consequently, he summoned lawyers from Moscow but said nothing about a will, claiming that he needed to consult them on several matters of business. Hard on their heels, however, came several doctors (in order to testify that Father had made his will being of sound mind), including a young doctor, one Mikhail Molchanov, whose studies had been sponsored by Father. (Later Mikhail Molchanov became a professor of neuropathology who under the Soviet regime treated the son of the famous Professor Timiryazev, whose bust stands at the top of Tverskoy Boulevard in Moscow.)

Father spent several days closeted in his study with these guests, and everybody guessed that he was composing his will. Those "old retainers" who had never become reconciled to Mother were thrown into turmoil and went around grim-faced as they whispered in the corridors: they feared that "their duchess" would be left nothing and her children (Father's granddaughters) would be passed over, too. Mama was well aware that a number of the servants had resumed correspondence with the duchess behind her back.

Just as he seemed to be a little on the mend, the illness that was to take Father's life crept up unexpectedly. It was a creeping inflammation of the lungs, accompanied by a slight temperature, a feeling of weakness, and occasional bouts of shivering. At that time, Mother was pregnant for the second time—with me.

The slight temperature was dismissed by doctors as the result of a cold or just nerves, but it had a debilitating effect. Finally, he developed a dry cough. Mama was very alarmed and insisted that they go to Moscow, where Father could be examined by leading doctors.

As Father had sold the Moscow residence, they stayed at the Loskutnoy Hotel, and later, when Father showed no signs of improvement, Mama hired the Kharuzin house on Sobachaya Square. This was an old, two-story house, big enough to house them and their servants.

Father knew he was dying and did his best to prepare Mother to continue without him. But nothing that he and a whole bevy of doctors could say seemed able to persuade the young woman to evince any desire to live, not even for the sake of the child she was carrying. She paid no heed to her unborn child. When Father took to his bed for good, she refused to leave his side day or night and, finally, weakened, would doze leaning against the head of the bed. Usually she just sat there, holding her husband's head in her lap. Whenever he seemed to sink into oblivion, she would start to weep until the child in her womb, as though sensing its mother's distress, would start to thrash around in a kind of frenzy. The doctors told her straight out that if she did not take care and gave way to desperation, there was little chance that her baby would be born alive. She waved them away. Even though there was always a nurse on duty beside Father's bed, she refused to leave his room and even had her meals brought there.

At that time Mama received a visit from Countess Sophia Sergeevna Ignatieva (the mother of Lieutenant-General Alexei Ignatiev, author of *Fifty Years in the Ranks*). She was born Princess Meshcherskaya, the daughter of my father's brother Sergei, so she was my cousin. She had traveled down from Petersburg in the hope of arranging a reconciliation between Father and his daughter and to persuade him to lift the curse he had placed on her. Yet again, his weakened voice whispered a categorical "Never!" and the countess left without achieving her aim.

A week before his death, Father said to Mama, "Katya, I beg you not to succumb to despair. I feel certain that the child I shall never see will be a daughter. Call her Catherine. She will look like me, so that will be a comfort to you. When I die, take my favorite sapphire ring off my finger and keep it for her. Give it to her when she turns sixteen and tell her to wear it always."

Seeing that Father was sinking fast, Mama sent the duchess a telegram without saying anything to Father about it. She still hoped that she would be able to persuade, to entreat Father into forgiving his daughter. But due to a series of unforseen difficulties, the duchess was unable to travel immediately and arrived too late to see her Father alive. In fact, she arrived after the funeral, so all she could do was attend several memorial services.

Father was fully conscious before he died. He blessed Mama and his small son and also embraced and thanked young Doctor Molchanov. "Thank you, my friend," he said to him. "You did everything you could, and I trusted you more than all the professors put together. I have a last request: look after Katya!"

Molchanov was Mama's doctor for the rest of her life, and, when I grew up, he treated me, too. However, I finally stopped going to him because he refused to accept any payment from me for his services.

Even after Father's heart and breathing had stopped, Mama would not accept that he had died. She sat by his side, clinging to his hand until it turned cold. After that, Mama collapsed into deep unconsciousness. The doctors took advantage of this and, as soon as she began to come round, gave her a sleeping draught, so that sleep—even one induced by medicine—would give her nerves a period of respite. Furthermore, those hours of sleep spared her the sight of all those preparations which must be carried out before the body of the deceased can be put into the coffin.

Nevertheless, when she awoke after hours of drugged sleep, her first wish was to see her husband's body. She was assisted out of bed and into the hall, where the coffin had been placed. When she saw her dead husband, she succumbed to a nervous collapse, and her legs gave way, paralyzed. The doctors hurried to check my fetal heartbeat, but it seemed to have disappeared. The consensus of opinion was that the baby had died. It was established later that the sudden paralysis which had affected Mama's legs caused a shock, which resulted in my being born with a congenital cardiac insufficiency. That was why the fetal heartbeat was so weak that the doctors could not trace it. Believing the fetus to be dead, the doctors wanted to do an immediate Caesarian section to save Mama's life. She refused to let them. "Leave me alone!" she said to them. "My husband has died, and I want to die, too!" The doctors refused to be paid off or to leave. They finally left only when Mother gave them a written statement, absolving them of any responsibility and affirming that she had refused to let them operate on her. She was just as deaf to the pleas of her mother, her sisters, and her brothers.

"I want to die," she said, over and over. "Leave me to die with the baby, which is already dead anyway! I have nothing to live for!"

In accordance with family tradition, my father was buried at the main Meshchersky estate, Lotoshino, which was held by Father's older brother, Boris, and then went to his son, Sergei Borisovich Meshchersky. When the body was taken out of the house, the following incident occurred. Mama did not wish to take her little son to the funeral; she felt he was too young to understand and would only be left with frightening memories. So Vyacheslav saw the funeral procession leave the Kharuzin house from the window of his nursery on the second floor. With him were his nurse, his governess, and our old majordomo, Alexei Ivanovich. In order to distract the little boy, Alexei Ivanovich said to him, "You see, little prince, we won't be calling you 'little' any longer. You were little while your father Alexander Vasilyevich was alive, but from now on you are the prince, and we will call you Your Highness!"

"No, no, Alexei!" responded the child. "You don't understand anything! I'm only *sort of* a prince!"

"What do you mean?" asked all the adults, surprised.

"Because first of all I have to grow up, then go to war, and after I get shot through the lungs two times, like Papa, *then* I'll be a real prince!"

This declaration finally came to the ears of my grandfather. He had been very ill for a long time and was too ill either to travel to comfort his favorite daughter in her loss or to attend the funeral. When he heard about Vyacheslav's avowal, however, he was delighted.

"How happy I am," he cried, "that this small child already

realizes that the most sacred duty of anyone in this life is to defend his homeland!"

Mama returned to Vesely Podol after Father's funeral, but continued to rent the Kharuzin house in Moscow. She had still not regained the use of her legs and had to be taken everywhere in a wheelchair. She wanted to see her father very much, but had no idea why he did not come to her. She kept hoping that he would come to Vesely Podol, and the rest of the Podborskys kept assuring her that he would, just as soon as he felt a little stronger; but in the meantime, they said, his heart was acting up, and it would be foolish for him to undertake a long journey. At the same time, Grandfather was worrying desperately about his favorite daughter, yearned to see her and offer her moral support and advice. . . . He knew her generosity and feared that this generosity would leave her penniless. Here are some extracts from his last letters to her:

My kind daughter Katya! What a terrible array of coincidences: on September 29, my brother and your uncle, Ivan Semyonovich, so beloved by all of us, died. On December 22, we lost your husband, our dear Prince Alexander Vasilyevich, and I fear that I, too, am not long for this world . . ."

And then, with all the sincerity of his truthful nature, he went on to warn her about the rest of the family, putting Mama on her guard: "In such a time of grievous loss and heartbreak, one frequently feels that everything is worthless. It may well be that among the people surrounding you now—be they distant or *very close*—there are some who will cast greedy eyes upon that to which they have no right, who will take advantage of your mood to ask for gold ornaments with precious stones, be they rightfully yours or the child's. Perhaps the child you carry beneath your heart will be a little daughter. So hold on to all the valuables; do not give them away . . ."

Further, Grandfather included advice concerning a lawyer, and then, as if feeling his own impending death, he sent her his blessing: "May the Lord God bless you, my dear daughter Katya, just as I, your father, bless you . . ." He also added a few lines addressed to his grandson: "May the Lord also bless my kind, humble, truthful, bright, and clever-minded Slavochka, my beloved grandson, as I, his grandfather, bless him. May he be strong and respectful and loving toward his mother, and obedient to her wishes. May he grow to serve the state and society, and be a comfort to his mother."

Grandfather died on January 2, several days after this last letter to Mama. This was the ultimate blow for her. All she did for days on end was read and reread all the letters she had ever had from her "dearest ones"—that is, from her father and husband—whose deaths had come so close to one another. Grandfather left a will in his faultless copperplate handwriting, but there was really nothing for him to leave. The only article he had ever had of any worth—the gold watch given to him by the tsar—was stolen by his enterprising daughter Olga when she eloped. I must add that, when Mama carried out Father's wish and removed his favorite sapphire ring from his finger, she was amazed to see that two other rings he usually wore were gone. "Oh, those!" exclaimed the same enterprising Olga. "Don't search for them, Cath, I've got them. I took them as a keepsake from the prince." And so she had, with all the speed of a grave robber, when Mama had fainted after Father died. One of the rings she had pulled off his still-warm hand was valuable from an historical point of view: it had belonged to Emperor Paul I and was given by him to one of the Meshcherskys; it was a ring denoting a Master of a Masonic Lodge (it is widely known that Emperor Paul was a Mason). The ring was of pure gold and in the form of a "Gordian knot."

Grandfather's will is interesting because of the charges he

places on his family. The unpretentious nature of the funeral for which he asks is not so much due to his poverty but to his strict sense of propriety. He died without having so much as once accepted a penny from his daughter and had no desire to benefit from his son-in-law's wealth. His will commences as follows:

In the name of the Father, the Son, and the Holy Ghost. Amen. Feeling that the day of my death is at hand, my wishes and requests are that I be buried in accordance with our slender means, as simply and as economically as possible. That the funeral service be conducted only by a priest, a deacon, a reader, and one assistant; we cannot afford the expense of a choir. My coffin should be a simple wooden one, painted to resemble oak, with ordinary metal clasps and fastenings. I should wish my grave to be in a new, visible part of the cemetery, if possible—near a tree, and not a plot already surrounded by numerous tombstones, by agreement with the foreman of the grave diggers . . .

He ends his will thus:

I call upon you all to live in mutual love, friendship, harmony, and understanding. Should any quarrels, differences of opinion or other strife occur—put an end to them as soon as they start, do not let them grow and develop. Treat those around you with good will and respect. Avoid malicious words and gossip among yourselves and with others: if you cannot stop such talk, then walk away from it. Judge not, lest ye be judged. My silver doctor's watch is to be wound daily and hung on the wall near the icons and sanctuary lamp, so that the light of the lamp and the ticking of the watch can remind you that as well as the physical world around you there is also another, unseen world, into which pass the souls of the deceased.

At the same time, a new storm was about to break over Mama's head. All efforts to find Father's will proved fruitless. It had simply disappeared. In other words, it had been stolen by some of the servants, who had maintained a vigil near the room in which Father lay dying and used the confusion following immediately upon his death to remove and destroy his will. They even set about rumors that many of Father's friends had come to see him as well as doctors and that he had not said a word about a will to any of them.

The duchess was back in Moscow, gathering evidence of some kind and searching for witnesses. Then she traveled to Petersburg to lodge petitions or the like. She threatened to publish an alleged clandestine romantic correspondence between Mother and Paolo Trubetskoy, and this gave rise to yet another slander against Mama—that Vyacheslav was Trubetskoy's illegitimate child. The "evidence" for this lie was supposed to be the circumstance that my brother was dark-haired and dark-eyed. Some people professed to believe this shameless libel; others said they didn't. But in their hearts, everyone must have known that the duchess's latest allegation was a falsehood, because Vyacheslav was already four years old when Mama met Trubetskoy for the first time on his visit to Vesely Podol. The duchess was demanding the greater part of the inheritance, stressing that her mother, Elizaveta Stroganova, had brought Father an enormous dowry when they married, and because of this she and her children had a legitimate claim on the estate.

Mama remained totally indifferent to this new scandal. "I'm going to die soon, anyway," she said, "and Slavchik, as the male heir, will get something, whatever the outcome, and that is enough. As for me—I don't want anything!"

And she left for Vesely Podol, convinced that she carried the means of her death inside her—a dead fetus. Great concern, however, was felt by Grandmother and by those friends who had come to know and love Mother and who had been in favor of her marriage with Father. The court case initiated by the duchess attracted an immense amount of interest, especially among the press, which is always keen for a sensation. Not just Moscow, but also Petersburg awaited the court hearing with avid curiosity. The duchess pinned her hopes on the weak, indecisive, and frequently contradictory nature of Tsar Nicholas II.

The Prince's Legacy

And now I come to an "historical" event in the life of the Meshcherskys, one which was much discussed and exclaimed over at the time.

The Meshcherskys and the Podborskys were always deeply religious. In our frequently hard and bitter life, Mama and I were invariably sustained by faith and prayer: we always felt that alongside our ordinary, mortal existence there was a parallel life on another plane. Yet frequently these two planes of existence would intersect and relieve the gray tedium of our days with truly amazing occurrences. The hand of Providence would reverse events, giving us a totally new direction.

Vesely Podol was plunged into mourning. The flag on the Meshchersky heraldic tower flew at half-mast, and dimmed lanterns burned at the entrance to the main drive. Life continued unabated, and lights burned in the right wing of the palace. Although all social gatherings had been canceled, neighbors from surrounding estates came to pay their respects to the young widow, and they had to be housed for several days, something that pleased the Podborskys greatly.

Mama was practically out of her mind with grief and did not want to see anyone. She refused to leave her room even for meals and lived like a recluse in the left wing of the palace. The central wing of the palace, which was used for balls and receptions, was completely dark, all the blinds drawn day and night. Therefore visitors would proceed straight to the right wing, where they were greeted enthusiastically by my uncles, Nikolai and Dmitri, and my aunts, Olga and Anatolia.

With no dances or picnics to enliven their existence, Mama's relatives amused themselves by riding, setting off in a noisy cavalcade across the countryside; or, if the weather was inclement, they played cards, recited poetry, and rehearsed plays they intended to stage as soon as the year of mourning was over. Olga, of course, was the driving force behind all these diversions.

Mama, in the meantime, gave up praying and veiled all the icons in her wing of the palace. She took off the cross from around her neck. All night she would kneel before the large portrait of the prince, the one he had given her all those years ago. "I prayed to him," she wrote in her diary. "I prayed to him to take me to him as quickly as possible, otherwise I would take my life myself. Only when I die will I believe in the existence of God and life beyond the grave." In her desperation, pleading with the portrait of her dead husband, she would weep, then moan, and then fall into a kind of stupor. Every morning Nanny Pashenka would find the young woman, lying stiff and cold on the floor. Luckily nobody but Pashenka dared enter Mother's rooms, so nobody else witnessed her strange behavior. Nanny was too frightened to say anything to Grandmother, because she feared that doctors would be called and the word would go out that the young princess had gone mad. Pashenka also kept quiet because she believed that Mother's illness was a temporary series of hysterical fits, which would pass with time. But Mother, at this time, was writing in her diary, "I do not believe that God exists and will believe in Him only if He sends me death and lets me join my dead husband."

One evening the Podborskys returned from a highly enjoyable soirée at the estate of our neighbors, the Counts Gudima-Levkoviches, and went off to bed. Aunt Olga retired very pleased with herself: the sounds of music and the compliments addressed to her still rang in her ears. She lay in her warm, soft bed, reliving her evenings successes.

Suddenly she noticed that the sanctuary lamp in front of the icon of the Virgin Mary in the corner began to flicker strangely, first almost dying out, then flaring up again. Aunt Olga was just about to stretch out her hand for the bellpull to summon a maid to adjust the lamp when it flickered once more and started burning strongly and evenly with a peculiar blue light, which illuminated the whole room like strong moonlight. At the same time, she was filled with a fear which held her immobile and incapable of reaching for the bellpull. Then a thin stream of something that looked like white smoke began to trickle intò the room through the keyhole and soon formed a large cloud which swayed before her bed and seemed to emit a low moan. Then the cloud grew smaller and denser, finally resolving itself into the tall, thin form of the late prince. When he spoke, his voice did not come from the apparition but seemed to be right beside her ear, striking terror into her heart, for it was as though the ghost had bent right down to her.

"Go to Katya immediately!" commanded the apparition. "Go to her at once and tell her to stop blaspheming. She has fallen into great sin, and she must atone for it with a great deal of prayer. Tell her that her tears, her misery, and her grief are binding me to the earth with heavy chains. It is very hard for me, and all that can help me is prayer. Tell Katya that she is to go to the tower, to the round knights' room. There, in the carved Italian table, she will find that which is vital to her . . ."

The sanctuary lamp went out, and the room was plunged into darkness. With shaking hands, Olga found her dressing gown and fled from the room, bumping into furniture in her hurry and screaming at the top of her voice. Everyone in the palace was up and on their feet within the next quarter of an hour. Olga succumbed to hysterics, demanding that every room in the palace be illuminated. Large flaming torches were lit, and a whole procession wound its way to the left wing in which Mother was closeted. Muted light shone feebly from her windows. Aunt Olga burst into Mama's bedroom like a hurricane and flung herself at numerous portraits and pictures of Father, turning them to face toward the wall.

"What are you doing here?" she shrieked at Mama. "What on earth are you up to? Black magic? Witchcraft?! What valuables has he hidden in the knights' room? He's just appeared to me with an order to go there! Tomorrow I want you to order up some horses for us; my husband and I won't stay another day in this accursed palace!"

Everyone rushed off to the tower and crowded into the knights' room. The Italian table, brought by my great-grandfather from Florence, stood dainty and polished on its carved legs. It had no drawers.

"You must have had too much champagne," said Mama in a tired voice. But for the first time since Father's death, the flicker of a smile crossed her face.

"No, no!" insisted Olga with mounting agitation. "I'm not going to let you out of this room! There must be a drawer, do you hear me, the prince said so! Do you want that ghost coming back and haunting me? He won't leave me in peace now, and I'll die of a heart attack!"

At first, examination of the table yielded no results, but then Mama slid her hand along the lacelike carving which ran around all four sides of the table and felt two incisions in the wood, skilfully concealed by the carpenter's art. She tugged lightly at the wood between the incisions, and a small secret drawer opened, smoothly and easily. Inside was a sealed second copy of the prince's will, duly signed and witnessed. He must have guessed that his first, official will would be stolen and destroyed, and he died before he got around to telling his wife of the existence of this copy.

Father's will was a lengthy document in which he explained in detail why he was leaving nothing to his daughter by his first marriage: she had received her share in her dowry when she married Duke Sasso-Ruffo and left Russia. Father acknowledged that his first wife had been immensely wealthy by her own wish and had the Stroganov part of the inheritance included in the duchess's dowry. Father even listed this Stroganov property, including the famous "royal" diamonds given to his wife by that Nikolai Stroganov who had married a Romanov princess. Father also noted his own wedding present to the newly married pair: before visiting them in Italy for the first time, he had purchased a small seaside villa with a plot of land on the shore of the Mediterranean. He named this villa Lily's House, and stayed in it whenever he came to Italy. I had confirmation of this in 1950 from my nephew Alexei Ignatiev. He expressed disapproval of what he felt was my father's "stupid wilfullness," and added, "He was an 'incorrigible Russian,' your father. He always referred to his son-in-law as 'that dago' behind his back, and Lily's House only came to be because every time your father came to Italy, he didn't want to walk on Italian soil but on his own Russian property!"

In his will, Father reiterated the curse he had placed on his daughter and left everything to his second wife—my mother.

After this miracle with the copy of the will, Mother came to her senses, went to confession and Holy Communion, and had requiem services celebrated frequently in the palace chapel. If one thinks carefully about what happened, one can see clearly the merciful Hand of God. What would have occurred if the ghost of the prince had not appeared to Olga, the most buoyant and egotistical of them all, but to Mother? Surely she would have lost her sanity. Nobody returned to bed on that memorable night when the copy of the prince's will was discovered. Grandmother sent an urgent telegram to Moscow to halt the court proceedings, and the next morning she set out for Moscow with her eldest son, Nikolai, to present the copy of the prince's will, which completely overturned all the duchess's claims.

As was to be expected, the duchess claimed that the copy presented was a forgery. Specialists were convened; lawyers were present; Father's signature was checked; but the matter was finally decided by those who had witnessed Father's will and came forth to testify that the copy found in the knights' room was genuine. Without any further court proceedings, all Father's property was ceded to Mama and Vyacheslav. However, in view of Mother's youth and inexperience, the nobility appointed a trustee—Sergei Borisovich Meshchersky, the son of Father's older brother.

Even before returning to Vesely Podol from Moscow, Mama suddenly regained the use of her legs and was able to abandon the wheelchair. She was very weak but could get around with the aid of a walking stick. She was under constant medical scrutiny, but the doctors could detect no signs of the blood-poisoning they had predicted when she refused to have her unborn child removed.

Having secured the inheritance, Mama, with characteristic generosity and decency, instructed the bank to make over a large sum of money to the prince's three granddaughters as a "present." She also sought a reconciliation with the duchess, but the meeting failed in its purpose. Mama was very shaken by it and unexpectedly went into normal labor.

I was born very weak, and Mama hovered between life and death for three days. When doctors offered surgical intervention, however, she refused. I survived only because Nature herself protected me. I was inside a "double placenta," one of which had collapsed and was wrapped about my body, while the other one had remained whole. One could say that I was "born lucky."

The doctor who supervised my birth was another of Father's protégés, Mikhail Molchanov's brother Vasili, who later became a famous pediatrician. It was he who determined immediately that I had a congenital cardiac insufficiency.

Mama remembered the promise made to her by Father John of Kronstadt and wrote to him immediately. He did not write back but came to see her personally. It was early spring, and the whole family was at the Petrovskoye estate. Father John baptized me in the small, warm winter church of the Protection of the Holy Veil, which had been built by my father. My godparents were Count Alexei Olsufyev and Countess Alexandra Miloradovna; the servant's room and laundry of her former house on Povarskaya Street are where I live today.

Such are the events which preceded my birth. The indifference my mother felt toward me, thinking me dead even while she carried me in her womb, remained with her all her life. Had I been capable of understanding my surroundings when I first opened my eyes, I would have seen that everything around me spoke of deep mourning. Because I was born after my father's death, Grandmother called me *Oeuvre posthume* (posthumous creation) as a joke. When I was brought to my mother for the first time, as she lay exhausted and drained, she waved the nurses aside without interest, and said sadly, "My son Slavik was a child of joy, but this one is a child of grief!" These painful words of my mother's were my start in life.

Part III
Epilogue

$\mathcal{A}$nd in this fashion my mother and I completed our "baptism by hard work." After hearing the rare beauty of my mother's voice by chance at a local concert, the workers of Rublevo sent her off to Moscow: "Take the qualification tests at RABIS [the professional association for the arts] and teach our children to sing the way you do," they said. We were issued the necessary papers to re-establish our Moscow residence permit in apartment No. 5 at 22 Povarskaya (nowadays Vorovskovo) Street.

One might think that we had now entered upon a new life, and that nothing more is left for me say. Alas, such was not the case. The Bolsheviks had their own view of the arts. The Moscow Conservatory, which had trained so many brilliant musicians, was now located in a side wing, the Small Hall, and the main buildings of the Conservatory had been turned into a cinema, with a huge sign outside: "The Colossus." The symphony orchestra had been disbanded as a bourgeois relic, and the conductor was dismissed—for the same reason, I suppose. In its place, the Communists created a body called the "Persimfans," the first symphony orchestra without a conductor. It was supposed to conduct itself, in some way, but the idea was a failure, and it soon ceased to exist. The Palace of Culture was located on Vozdvizhenskaya Street in the beautiful former mansion of the Morozov merchant family, and a large sign, "Proletcult," hung at its entrance. Muscovites shook their heads as they passed by, saying sadly, "Farewell to culture!" The Soviet press proudly called upon the populace to "burn Raphaels, demolish museums, and trample the flowers of culture in the name of our future!" On the Manezhnaya Square, near the Kutafyev Tower, stark naked couples strolled beside the cast-iron railings of the Alexander Gardens. They all sported bright red sashes across their shoulders bearing the words "Down with Shame!" Endless searches and arrests led to the expulsion of born Muscovites from the capital, while new faces flooded in from other towns and the provinces. Lenin's dictum that "any cook can become head of state" had received wide publicity. . . .

My mother taught at the Conservatory for one year only. Then one of the meetings at the Conservatory was attended by the sister of the poet Valeri Bryusov. A mountain of a woman, dressed in an old leather coat and cap which never left her head, she heaved her bulk up onto the stage, grunting and wheezing from the exertion. Unclenching the short, fat fingers of her enormous hand, she flung down a huge, bulging old briefcase on the dais, and glared at everyone present with her large, bleary, bulging eyes.

"Comrades!" she cried compellingly. "Comrades! How has it come to pass that our honest, working Communist circle has been penetrated by a real princess, a capitalist spy? She has not just penetrated our ranks peripherally, but has managed to get herself onto the staff! Who has entrusted the training of our young people to this woman? She's a fascist, and uses singing lessons as a cover to teach them the fascist Italian language! Throw her out, I say! Throw her out!"

And my mother sat there, sadly recalling the years when

she studied under such famous masters as Guerci, Mazetti, Bimboni and Massini. "The voice is a thing of beauty and integrity," they said. "It cannot live in an attic (that is, behind a mask), nor can it draw power from the basement (the diaphragm). The voice must dip and fly like a butterfly; it's like a kiss on the lips. . . ."

Mama was dismissed amid uproar, her RABIS membership card was withdrawn, and instead she was issued a work permit enabling her to engage only in manual labor.

The relevant department of the Moscow Executive Council gave her a spade, and sent her to the outskirts of the city to shovel rotten apples into trucks. In the unbelievably unsanitary conditions of this work, Mama contracted typhus and had to be rushed to the hospital in an ambulance.

Our life on Povarskaya Street was not all roses, either. We found ourselves surrounded by the very same political commissars who had only recently thrown us out into the street, and who were still in the process of selling off our former possessions, such as gold-framed mirrors, beautiful crystal chandeliers, rare porcelain, and the like.

Our main and mortal enemy was the political commissar Fyodor Stepanovich Alekseyev, who had robbed us of the contents of our dining room and drawing room. He wrote countless denunciations and reports about us, and he sat on the military tribunal which tried me. Luckily, I managed to get off, even though he had me brought to the tribunal under armed guard. However, he had no trouble gathering signatures to a petition from all the Communists in the building, which resulted in our being forced to move into the former watchman's quarters in the courtyard. The place had no heating or amenities of any kind, apart from a reeking sink in one corner. The lavatory was in another building, and we would have to cross the yard in sleet or snow to use it. That one lavatory, opening directly onto the stairs, had to be used by everyone and cleaned. Deprived of all our rights, Mother and I felt a painful kind of attachment to our tiny hovel, seeing it as a fragment of our homeland which remained ours in spite of everything. Later it was to become a refuge for my mother's older sister Olga and her husband, and her younger sister Anatolia. We also took in a young student composer who suffered from a lung disease and had nowhere to live. We were crammed in like sardines, but the fact that all these people lived there ensured that the watchman's quarters remained our pied-à-terre for life.

After Mother was thrown out of the Conservatory, I was soon dismissed from my job in a kindergarten which I had opened in partnership with my old nurse's niece, A. G. Telegina. I lost my post after we were visited by an unusually "vigilant" state inspection committee that asked the children which of their teachers they liked best.

"Auntie Kitty," they chorused.

"And why is that?"

"Because she wears lace dresses and has diamonds on her fingers!"

The committee immediately began looking into my antecedents, and I was fired within twenty-four hours.

When I was eighteen, I passed all the tests and was accepted into the Operetta Theater. In order to avoid problems over the issue of my social origins, I decided to try for the job in a factory, and was taken on as an apprentice in the Rosa Luxemburg textile works. I started off with winding, then went on to more complicated work, and finally received a master's qualification on weaving machines. In fact, I did so well I was nominated as top candidate to the Central Scientific-Experimental Station. But that summer we went on a factory excursion to the woods along my native Kiev Highway, and I was recognized by several of our former milkmaids, who happened to be traveling in the same railway carriage.

"The princess! The princess! Our princess!" they cried, rushing up to embrace me. As a result, that year I was arrested as a "capitalist agent in disguise." . . .

But the worst was when they started to try to recruit me as an informer for the Lubyanka secret police. If I had agreed, then after my first arrest I would have been released and enjoyed a carefree life and lacked for nothing in exchange for my honor.

I have never forgotten my first meeting with an investigator.

"What's this?" he said. "You're wearing evening shoes? It's about minus twenty degrees outside right now, isn't it? Well, we'll keep you in those shoes, and load you into a freight train straight for Siberia to cut logs near the Yenisey River. . . . Of course, it's always possible that you'll freeze to death en route, like some of your other fellow passengers. Usually we just dump the corpses from the train: we're very humane, we don't make the living travel with carrion. . . . So what do you choose—life or death? The only way you can get out of here alive is by becoming one of our agents."

And so "it" began. My life was invaded by an inhuman beast of an investigator from the Special Section, which was housed in a lovely green-and-white building inside the Lubyanka grounds. Let us call this investigator "Ivan Ivanovich." He held me in detention for three months only, and then released me after making me sign an undertaking that nobody, not even my mother, was to know the substance of our discussion. Naturally I signed this paper, then went home and told my mother and husband everything. I knew full well that, willy-nilly, I had embarked on a perilous course, but I could see no other way out. If I had gone before a firing squad, I would have sealed my mother's fate, too, because they would have packed her off to the Solovki camps so that she wouldn't make a nuisance of herself with demands and petitions. And I must admit that I did not want to die. . . . I could feel instinctively that Ivan Ivanovich nursed some special hatred toward me. He tightened his tentacles around me like a giant octopus, and applied every means at his command to recruit me. Well, I took up the challenge. The head of the Special Section had already entered my name on a list of those destined for the camps, and gave Ivan Ivanovich a limited time to recruit me. So Ivan Ivanovich set to work.

"You have a weak heart, Ekaterina Alexandrovna," he remarked. "So I won't tell you how much time you have left to make up your mind. Who knows, you may go off and hang yourself in desperation, and rob me of the pleasure of taking your life myself. Still, I'll try to make a colleague of you. Whenever you get a postcard from me asking you to come around to the library, that will mean that you should telephone me at once, and we'll meet."

Actually I was much more afraid of Ivan Ivanovich's driver than of the investigator himself. The driver always wore a cap pulled down low over his forehead and swathed the lower part of his face in a large scarf. Every time he came to pick me up, I tried not to look at him as I got into the car, so he wouldn't think that I was trying to memorize his face. I can just imagine what kind of scenes he took part in. . . . It's impossible to describe all the ways in which Ivan Ivanovich tried to break me. Suffice it to say that he brought an enormous arsenal of psychological weapons into play. For instance, once he summoned me at ten o'clock in the evening. It had not yet iced over, but there was a strong wind and snow was falling.

"I want to take you for a drive," he declared jovially. "I've been up to my ears in work. I need a break. Let's drive out of town for a breath of fresh air."

We drove out onto the Minsk Highway, and Moscow was soon lost in the swirling snow.

"Stop here," commanded Ivan Ivanovich, rapping on the glass partition between us and the driver. We pulled over, and the driver sprang out nimbly to open the door for me. I got out, and immediately sank into a deep snowdrift. Ivan Ivanovich caught my arm solicitously, to keep me from falling over, and guided me out onto the road.

"Isn't this romantic?" he mused, drawing me along with him

and turning his head to peer into my face. "Night, falling snow, and here we are, strolling along like a pair of lovers!"

I kept my mouth shut, but Ivan Ivanovich continued blithely:

"Take a look over there, to your left. See that convoy of trucks making its way down that steep slope?"

There was, indeed, a line of trucks with huge lights, crawling slowly down an incline.

"As soon as they come up to us," proceeded Ivan Ivanovich conversationally, squeezing my elbow in a sudden, painful grip, "I'll just throw you under the first pair of wheels, and that will be that!"

I felt a rush of blood to my head: if the government has given this sadist the power of life and death over me, it doesn't mean that he can also humiliate and torture me like this! How long will this unbearable cat-and-mouse game go on? Isn't death by a bullet preferable? A few minutes of pain, and that's all . . . ?

I broke away from him and ran across to the other side of the road. Turning to face him, I tore open the buttons of my coat.

"Why wait for the trucks?" I shouted at him. "Don't you see how hard it's snowing? If I fall on my back into the ditch, I'll be completely covered by morning, and they won't find my body before spring. Well, come on, shoot! Or are you a liar and a pathetic coward, too?"

He crossed the road in two bounds, scooped me up bodily, like a kitten, and flung me back into the car.

"Insolent bitch!" he grated, collapsing onto the seat beside me. "I hate you! Why the hell did they force you onto me? I'm fed up with you!"

It seemed to me that he ground his teeth, and the veins on his forehead stood out like cords.

I did not feel frightened, but my nerves must have been shattered, because my whole body began to shake uncontrollably. I clenched my teeth as hard as I could to stop them from chattering. I pulled out a small bottle of my favorite lily-of-the-valley perfume from the pocket of my coat and shook a few drops on my handkerchief. So that Ivan Ivanovich would not be able to see my face, I began to fan myself with the handkerchief, pretending to be looking at something out of the window.

Much later I learned that women were tortured and even raped at the Lubyanka. Probably this happened to attractive women who tried to better their situation by flirting with their captors, thus arousing their base male instincts. Luckily the Lord did not endow me with good looks, nor was I at all disposed to coquetry, and I suppose this is what saved me from such a fate.

How have I managed to retain my optimism and buoyancy throughout my whole life? In the first place, through faith and prayer. In the second place, I have always enjoyed and found something interesting in any work I have had to do. I never had any real friends among women, and the ones I thought were my friends all betrayed me to one degree or another.

Of course, if my life had been nothing but an unending series of tragedies, my weak heart would have given out long ago. I lived by the feelings of people who were deeply devoted to me. People who hid me, time and again, who often risked their lives to help me even in the most terrible years of the Terror. It was male friendship that made me happy. Sometimes, in order to shield me from the ever-prying binoculars of the Lubyanka, men gave me the protection of their name, and this is the explanation for my many "fictitious" marriages (four in all). Once I had a very well-connected student whom I taught German. He was an important figure in the implementation of Lenin's electrification program. In the early postrevolutionary years, finding a place to live in Moscow was simply impossible. My student and his wife lived in a small room in a communal apartment. Suddenly, on the orders of Nadezhda Krupskaya, Lenin's wife, he was given a study in the huge Peoples' Commissariat for Education (NARKOMPROS) building near the Sretensky Gates where Krupskaya had her office, and which is preserved as a memorial to her to this day.

"Ekaterina Alexandrovna," he said to me, "here is the key to that study. Use it to lie low while they're still hunting you and badgering you with these constant summonses."

I could only shake my head sadly.

"You're very naive," I replied. "Do you really think that they won't run me to earth there?"

"They won't, you know!" laughed my friend Nikita Mikhailovich Krasovsky, a young director from the Moscow Arts Theater, who happened to be present. "I am asking for your hand in marriage here, in front of witnesses. We'll register as husband and wife, that'll take the wind out of their sails! Your mother can write an official statement for the house management here saying that you have disappeared without a trace. Well, what do you think of my idea? Not bad, is it?"

"Really, Nikita, you don't know what you're saying!" I expostulated. "I can't possibly allow you to make such a sacrifice. And what will happen if you fall in love with somebody?"

"That's out of the question right now, Kitty! I simply can't afford to fall in love. I'm working on two plays which must go on at all costs, so I won't be saving you, but, on the contrary, you'll be saving me! It will make it possible for me to flash my passport at all the ladies and tell them to abandon hope, because I'm a married man!" concluded Nikita gallantly. And so he saved me, like a true knight in shining armor.

I moved into my student's office block after officially becoming Ekaterina Krasovskaya. Mama came over frequently to stay the night, and when I went to Leningrad, she visited me there, too.

In the meantime, the bloody Stalinist "trials" were in full swing. In Leningrad I heard that 250 actors from the Moscow Arts Theater, including their director Nikita Krasovsky, had been sent out of Moscow. But the beacon of art shines through the darkness of slander, and Nikita, who settled into "voluntary exile" in sunny Alma-Ata, soon set up a small division of the Moscow Arts Theater. After a while he married. Fortunately Olga, his wife, was not an actress, but a faithful and loving wife. They were very happy.

The tempest of house searches, arrests, and executions did not bypass Leningrad: the friends I was living with were arrested, their apartment was sealed, and I returned to Moscow with a small suitcase, leaving the bulk of my possessions behind. I had no job and no hope of getting a residence permit. I found Mama in a very bad state. She had deliberately not mentioned in her letters that after yet another denunciation she had returned from prison into the care of the Pryanishnikov's, in the wooden house on Starokonyushenny Lane. But it wasn't much of a shelter. Several large trunks had been placed on top of each other in a vestibule, and on top of that was a large writing desk covered by a thin, old mattress. This is where my poor Mama had to sleep, right under the ceiling. After spending the whole day running around Moscow giving children music lessons, she would have to climb up a ladder to sleep on the desk which served as her bed.

And that was not all. The vestibule also housed another tenant, one Natalia Ivanovna Zhabrova. All that was left of her former youth and beauty were the gray curls which framed a face permanently bloated by drink. Her nose looked like a black hole in her face, and her eyes were rheumy and damp. Her voice was harsh and grating. She made her living by washing floors and got drunk every evening. Her hatred of the former upper classes verged on the pathological. She had a habit of rolling cigarettes out of newspaper and cheap shag tobacco, and would sit there, puffing clouds of foul-smelling smoke in Mother's direction, making her cough and choke. This would delight Zhabrova:

"Doncha like my tobacco, Yer Highness?" she would rasp.

"But yer 'Yer Lowness' now, ain't ya, so ya have ter get used to our proletarian ways!"

A former protégé of the Pryanishnikovs, one Vladimir Zakharovich Fokin, lived in a separate room in the building. He had known Mama for many years, and me since my birth. He committed a truly heroic act in exchanging his separate room with Zhabrova, and moved into the vestibule. He persuaded the other tenants to remove their trunks, bought Mama a bed and a little bedside table, and settled her in a corner with her icons, then rigged up a curtain so that she could have a measure of privacy. In this way he and Mother lived together, and I was moved to tears when I saw this peaceful and contented picture. So Mama's life was settled. And this is typical of the help and support we encountered.

However, I had no job, no residence permit, and not even a corner to call my own. But the Lord worked a miracle when one day, quite unexpectedly, I was embraced in the street by a gray-haired, blue-eyed lady. It was Elizaveta Andreyevna Krasovskaya.

"Kitty!" she cried. "My dear! I'll fix everything up for you! After all, I'm your mother-in-law, albeit fictitiously, but Soviet laws make it possible for me to have you registered for residence at my place, as my son's wife!"

Thanks to her generosity, I was able to live in Moscow at No. 51 Arbatskaya Street, just around the corner from Mama. But all these trials and tribulations would have undoubtedly ended in my death had I not been saved by . . . Ivan Ivanovich! I will do my best to reconstruct from memory the "confession" I once heard from his own lips.

"You know very well, Ekaterina Alexandrovna, that not only was I not attracted to you at all, but I really couldn't stand you. Then one day a colleague mentioned that he was handling the case of a husband and wife, Prince and Princess Meshchersky, who were being dispatched to the hard-labor camps. He gave me a look at their file, and to my amazement I saw that the wife was named Ekaterina Alexandrovna Meshcherskaya, born in 1904 [the same year I was born]. She turned out to be E. A. Fyodorova, the daughter of a royal lady-in-waiting. [E. A. Fyodorova ("Katya") had married my first cousin once removed, Ivan Sergeievich Meshchersky ("Vayka"), whose grandfather, Boris, was my father's brother. I had know Vayka and Katya since childhood.] I can't explain the feeling which gripped me, nor the reason for it, but I found myself hammering on my superior's door and demanding that your name be removed from the list of people to be liquidated, because you were apparently already headed for the camps.

" '*Apparently?*' he roared. 'What do you mean—*apparently?* Why didn't you make an end of her? Why did you drag your feet? How could she have passed right out from under your nose into the hands of another investigator, in another section of the building?' "

"He stared at me, flecks of foam on his lips. Opening a folder with a list of names on it, he slashed a line through yours. There was a moment of silence; then he spoke again, this time quite calmly and coldly:

" 'There are only a few days left before the October festivities. As soon as they're over, we will take up your personal case behind closed doors. I am sure you know what the charges against you will be!'

"I went back to my own office, which seemed to be very dark. I sat down in my chair and realized that someone else would be occupying it soon. And where would I be? Would I be at all? People frequently disappeared without a trace after hearings behind closed doors: 'died suddenly while performing his duty,' or something similar, would be the only explanation.

"Days and hours in which I did not live, but merely existed, dragged by. I continued working, but like a robot.

"As you know, we always hold rehearsals before any kind of state celebrations, usually at night to avoid impeding the city population and traffic. Traditionally we file through Red Square on horseback, like the cavalry. That fateful night, just as we came around the corner near the Historical Museum, my chief, the head of the Special Section, swayed in his saddle and then slid off his horse to the ground. Having lived the past few days in a state of unremitting dread, waiting for the ax to fall, I sat there like a stone, unable to make a move, while everybody else dismounted hurriedly and rushed over to help. But he was dead. The autopsy showed that he had died from a massive stroke. All I can remember is his outflung right hand, palm upward, as he lay there on the ground. The fingers were still bent, for only a few minutes before he had been gripping his horse's reins. Yet that hand had also held in its grip something else: two human lives—yours and mine. Nobody else will ever know this secret. . . . I suddenly recalled all your interminable stories about miracles, and felt myself break out in a cold sweat. Here it was—a *miracle!* And it had happened to me!"

When I told my friends about what he had said, they all cried, "He's not only a criminal and a sadist, he's an incorrigible liar to boot! You should be ashamed of yourself, Ekaterina Alexandrovna, for believing anything a creature like that told you! Vayka and Katya died in the camps anyway. How could you possibly believe that he destroyed or substituted any of your papers?"

After Stalin died and Khrushchev came to power, I was summoned to the Lubyanka again, to a section of the building and office that was not known to me.

A young, sprightly, and very cheerful-looking KGB officer guided me politely to a chair in front of his desk. He began by informing me that a new, benevolent time had come to the whole of the Soviet Union.

"And you, Ekaterina Alexandrovna," he announced, "are now totally in the clear. Clean as a whistle, and you can write that down everywhere!"

I looked at him as though he were mad and said nothing.

Why I had been "unclean" and what "dirt" I was now deemed to have shed remained a mystery to me. Guessing my perplexity, he continued:

"Of course, it is sad that you will not be able to embrace your brother again, because he died some years ago in a Kolyma concentration camp, but he has been posthumously cleared of the charges against him and fully exonerated. Now read this document and sign it."

He handed me a sheet of paper and indicated where I should sign. What brother were we talking about? I asked myself. My only brother, Vyacheslav, who organized an uprising in the Butyrskaya prison and escaped from a firing squad covered in blood, had been living in the U.S.A. for many, many years. . . . I looked at the paper and saw that it referred to Nikolai Alexandrovich Fyodorov, Katya's brother. So my file at the Lubyanka really had been destroyed, and all these years I had remained alive because it was thought that I was the long-dead Katya. The black wing of her death sheltered me, and it was all thanks to Ivan Ivanovich. He had not lied to me, after all. . . .

I signed the paper instead of the other Katya. As I did so, the memory of her straight, slender figure rose in my mind's eye, and I could not stop the tears running down my face. Of course, there was a significant difference between us: Katya had acquired her title through marriage; I have mine because I am the daughter of a prince. But the Bolsheviks still don't understand such fine distinctions, and thank God for it!

About the Author

EKATERINA ALEXANDROVNA MESHCHERSKAYA, now eighty-five, lives in Moscow in three cramped rooms of the former watchman's quarters of the same building where she and her mother had an apartment before the 1917 Revolution. Thanks to glasnost, she has had her memoirs (Part I of this book) published in a leading Soviet literary journal, *Novy Mir,* has been interviewed by the mass-circulation illustrated weekly *Ogonyek,* and has appeared on Soviet television. These days she is even commonly addressed as "Princess," once a term of obloquy.

Although because of her social origins she was arrested thirteen times, the last time after Stalin's death, and had to endure twenty-three house searches as well as countless denunciations, she remains free of bitterness.

Sustained throughout her perilous odyssey by her Russian Orthodox faith, by prayer, and by an unfailing commitment to do well at whatever task—however menial—she undertook, Ekaterina Meshcherskaya has earned the respect of her compatriots. Indeed, her courage, patriotism, and generosity of spirit could serve as models for any society.

Book Mark

The text of this book was set in a film version of the typeface
Weiss and the display in a version of Shelley Andante script by
Creative Graphics, Inc., Allentown, Pennsylvania.

This book was printed on 50-pound Glatfelter, an acid-free
paper, by Berryville Graphics, Berryville, Virginia.

Designed by Anne Ling